Communicating Hip-Hop

Communicating Hip-Hop

How Hip-Hop Culture Shapes Popular Culture

Nick J. Sciullo

 PRAEGER™

An Imprint of ABC-CLIO, LLC
Santa Barbara, California • Denver, Colorado

Library of Congress Cataloging-in-Publication Data

Names: Sciullo, Nick J. author.
Title: Communicating hip-hop : how hip-hop culture shapes popular culture / Nick J. Sciullo.
Description: Santa Barbara, California : Praeger, [2019] | Includes index.
Identifiers: LCCN 2018032422| ISBN 9781440842221 (cloth : alk. paper) | ISBN 9781440842238 (ebook)
Subjects: LCSH: Rap (Music)—Social aspects. | Hip-hop—Influence. | Popular culture.
Classification: LCC ML3918.R37 S3 2019 | DDC 306.4/84249—dc23
LC record available at https://lccn.loc.gov/2018032422

ISBN: 978-1-4408-4222-1 (print)
        978-1-4408-4223-8 (ebook)

23 22 21 20 19   1 2 3 4 5

This book is also available as an eBook.

Praeger
An Imprint of ABC-CLIO, LLC

ABC-CLIO, LLC
130 Cremona Drive, P.O. Box 1911
Santa Barbara, California 93116-1911
www.abc-clio.com

This book is printed on acid-free paper ∞

Manufactured in the United States of America

Contents

Preface

It is always difficult to attempt to capture a complex social phenomenon in a few pages, let alone to explain what it means in many different cultural arenas. Hip-hop was something I grew up with as a child in Virginia Beach, Virginia. Hip-hop was popular in my neighborhood, College Park, which was racially diverse. It sits roughly at the corner of three cities (Virginia Beach, Norfolk, and Chesapeake), so movement between different peoples with different experiences and different music preferences was the norm. Virginia Beach is a transient city with large populations of military personnel and tourists, making music and change a daily occurrence because music seemed to always inspire the rhythm of the region.

I grew up with the mid-1990s hip-hop, which includes the Fugees, Busta Rhymes, Tupac Shakur, Biggie Smalls, No Limit Records, Cash Money Records, Bone Thugs-n-Harmony, and other artists. The Hampton Roads region was and remains a hotbed of hip-hop activity, producing Timbaland, Missy Elliott, Nottz, Pharrell Williams and the Neptunes, and many other lesser known but still important artists. These artists played regularly in bars and clubs and on the radio. It would have been difficult to grow up in Virginia Beach and not be exposed to hip-hop.

My father grew up in Pittsburgh, exposed to a complex racial and ethnic environment where different racial and ethnic groups often found themselves in conflict for housing, jobs, and social services. Pittsburgh, a city of vibrant ethnic and racial minority communities, was a city very much in the center of hip-hop's politics even though we tend not to think of it as a hip-hop city. My father listened to the Motown greats and introduced me to them at an early age. I knew Stevie Wonder and Marvin Gaye early. Ray Charles was common as well. This may have been what most profoundly shaped my hip-hop listening experience. I understood, or at least thought I did, the tremendous problems with urban poverty, violence, and selective policing. Stevie Wonder's "Living for the City" told such a captivating story that it was impossible to resist its call for considering more seriously the impact of race and poverty in our cities.

Growing up in College Park, Virginia Beach, was exciting. There were many other children around, and they were from all over. They liked hip-hop, the alternative rock of the day, classic rock, and probably some country, although it was not very cool to like country in the neighborhood. Growing up, I was exposed to hip-hop because that seemed to be what everyone was listening to. MTV and BET still played mostly music videos, and many of them were hip-hop. Everyone seemed to pretend that they were a disc jockey (DJ) or an emcee. I would later try my hand at DJing in high school and college, mostly for my own stress relief but also because I was fascinated with creating and knew that the hip-hop pioneers of the Bronx and Brooklyn had parlayed these talents into flashy, financially lucrative careers.

My first memory as a DJ was trying to use a dual tape deck to produce scratching sounds. From there I incorporated Gemini 500s, a beginner turntable setup. I was fortunate in that my best friend's older brother was a DJ who was actually quite popular in the local radio and concert scene. I was terrified of asking him for help, but he agreed and helped me amass a great record collection. Because most of what I listened to was hip-hop and R&B, most of my DJing utilized these styles of music. I never fully accepted or really listened to electronica and its many derivations. Hip-hop was where my heart was.

Hip-hop, though, was about community back then more so than personal aggrandizement. It brought people together at a party or a barbeque. Lyrics were easy material as we tried our youthful hand at literary allusion. Knowledge of lyrics was a way to test who was cool or who might have a CD or cassette tape that you needed burned. Music sharing was popular then, and much of it happened via burning hard-copy CDs. Now the Internet enables this, much to the chagrin of many record companies but often to the delight of artists hoping to be discovered.

Hip-hop also provided the music to pump up competitors, and I would readily listen to it before high school debate competitions and swim meets. DMX was common in the same ways that people now might listen to Migos (me included) to get excited about their day or amped for a specific performance. Since I realized that hip-hop had this potential to motivate, to amplify one's emotions, this is probably where I began to think about hip-hop as a cultural phenomenon worth studying.

What kept me interested in hip-hop was how I saw it bringing people together. School dances featured more hip-hop than I'm sure administrators felt comfortable with. While middle school was full of awkwardness, high school was full of bump and grind, the rhythmic close-quarters dancing that many parents still abhor. And while the dancing was often sexual, it was also about a freedom of expression and a willingness to test boundaries and think about what the body and sound could do differently. A great beat would be the impetus that people needed to get to know one another, chat, dance, and laugh. Even a bad dancer could feel carried away by the music.

In college, I understood hip-hop and fell in with a group of rappers in suburban Richmond, Virginia. There were frequent freestyle competitions at a cool upstairs spot near what was the restaurant Sticky Rice in Richmond. I was never very good at freestyling, but I learned a lot from my emcee friends about the syntax of flowing. Of course, during this time street racing was also popular, so we would street race, battle rap, and try our best to figure out how someone became famous from hip-hop. That did not happen except for a show I performed in the bar at the University of Richmond's campus where I invited my rapper friends to perform; the bartender was forced to tell us multiple times to turn down the bass. It was there that I mixed in sounds of Southpark and other verbal jabs and exclamations to punctuate the live artists, earning their respect as a funny if not at least capable DJ.

In law school, I was fortunate enough to meet andré douglas pond cummings, one of the founders of hip-hop and law. I worked as his research assistant for two years. He studied hip-hop as an academic subject. Growing up in South Central Los Angeles at a time when gangsta rap was just what was happening, he had grown to appreciate N.W.A., Public Enemy, Tupac Shakur, and Snoop Dogg. Los Angeles was then and is now a hotbed of hip-hop activity, and cummings brought to law school an appreciation for the ways in which one's nonschool life could come to bear on one's school life. I had never really thought of hip-hop as something I could do as a scholar until then.

It was at that time that I began to understand hip-hop not just as the DJing of my youth. It was not simply culture but was also something to study. I worked on countless projects in law school and early in my academic career to think about and help others think about how important hip-hop is. This work also made me feel good in the sense that I felt I was writing and speaking about topics that mattered to people every day and not just in the hallowed halls of academia. I was doing real work in the sense that I was doing work that people would read and would help them understand what they did every day.

Most people interested in hip-hop have a similar story, and that is also what makes hip-hop interesting and relatable. It is about stories. Many of hip-hop's most memorable songs are stories. Although certainly not the most important, Eminem's "Stan" is just such a story. The song tells the story of an obsessed fan who takes Eminem's lyrics to heart, so much so that the fan becomes violently dangerous. The story is of course partly introspective, as Eminem reflects on the violence of his own lyrics, but is also a testament to the relationship that fans have to lyrics and how central hip-hop can be to their lives. Hip-hop stories are often introspective, but they also tell quite moving tales about struggle, structural racism, and the dangers of inner-city life. Ludacris's "Runaway Love" featuring Mary J. Blige tells the story of a young woman's harrowing journey through abuse and neglect of all types and her dogged determination to make something of herself in the world. Slick Rick's "Children's Story" exposes the dangers of crime and ends in a police chase, showing that hip-hop's reliance on narrative is one of its most attractive features and what keeps listeners and scholars eagerly engaged.

Although I have read many books on hip-hop, none really capture hip-hop culture or the complexities of hip-hop music appreciation. This book is an attempt to capture some thoughts about hip-hop in culture, which is important and meaningful. Hip-hop has never confined itself to one medium, so a book makes sense just as much graffiti on the side of a train or the art on someone's burned CD does. Hip-hop is everywhere, and I have felt this in all that I do. No matter where I travel in the United States or in the world, people are talking about hip-hop, and the music is everywhere.

People often ask me to rank my favorite artists or my favorite albums. I like artists for different reasons. Wyclef Jean was always profoundly important to me and was the first artist I wrote about in a scholarly article. I grew up listening to the Fugees, and *The Score* is still one of the most important hip-hop albums of all time. *The Score* introduced collaborations between reggae stars and hip-hop artists and featured sound production with beats that still stand the test of time. The album was overtly political and masterfully put metaphor to work. All of this has made *The Score* a fantastic album. I like both Tupac and Biggie, although I've spent more time studying Tupac. There is a lot to unpack in Tupac's music that isn't in Biggie's, but Biggie has some classic beats that encourage one to think about sitting in a lawn chair in a friend's driveway or garage just thinking about what possibilities the night might hold.

Ludacris is one of my favorites because he's so stylistically gifted. He possesses tremendous cadence and rhythm. Every remix he is on including collaborations with R&B artists seems to pop. I love remixes, particularly ones that combine R&B and rap, because I grew up at a time when the slow jam was a high school dance classic. In terms of older rap, Kool G Rap is underrated. Even his newer stuff is tremendously powerful. I loved the late great Craig Mack, whose delivery was fantastic. Rakim and Scarface, both very different artists, offer unforgettable bars at almost every juncture. I wish deeply that Big L had lived longer than his 24 years. He had a masterful flow and no doubt many albums beyond *Lifestylez ov da Poor & Dangerous*.

I also like trap music, in part because I spent four years in Atlanta and also because I grew up dancing and going to clubs. Music that made you move was important to me and still is. I have a deep love for Migos, Kevin Gates, Lil Jon, and other artists who produce the types of music that get people moving.

Music that brings people together is important, and while it is easy to hold up the socially conscious music that many scholars rally behind, it is equally as important to recognize the music that brings people together every day in clubs, on street corners, and at parties. One of the most important aspects of hip-hop music is that you can both respect and love Common and also appreciate the much different stylings of Lil John. Hip-hop is a diverse cultural form that recognizes many different types of talent and appreciates countless musical styles.

One need not be all in and reject whatever does not fit. Caring about hip-hop does not mean rejecting everything that is not hip-hop. Hip-hop hardliners will often argue that those who like other types of music are not really "hip-hop," as if diverse interest make people somehow less of a community member. This happens in the academy, where scholars who publish outside of their discipline or who collaborate with scholars in other departments are often derided as not committed to their own discipline at the same time as their colleges or universities promote interdisciplinary majors and PhD programs. It can be tough to fit in when such gatekeepers seem to keep the gates closed. Hip-hop is no different. For everyone who gets excited about people in the midwestern United States listening to and making hip-hop, just as many people seem to think that the only rap worth anything is in New York. This book does not take that approach, and it is something that I have always found strange especially when the diversity of ideas and styles that make everything from scholarship to fashion to education are what we ought to be after. I was fortunate to grow up listening to both Biggie and Tupac as well as Stevie Wonder, Creedence Clearwater Revival, and Queen. I was influenced by my peers and my father, and that helped me think broadly about music and the diverse influences and ideas that made music great. People interested in studying hip-hop should keep an open mind.

This book provides a number of references to artists and ideas. Many are explored here, but one should also read other books and articles featured in the "Further Reading" sections. One book will never capture everything about a subject, so in the spirit of the remix and the mash-up, take the pieces you like from this book, combine them with the art show you went to last week and the mixtape you just downloaded, and bring those to the table when you read one of the many other great books on hip-hop. It is only with those sorts of combinations that one begins to really understand how hip-hop is not just what is on the radio at a given time. Rather, hip-hop is all of these things.

Hip-hop is also about making do with what one has. DJs didn't always have the newest computer programs or the finest-engineered turntables. Sometimes all they had were two tape decks. Rappers didn't have studio time and ready access to a Roland TR-808 (a premium drum machine). So, this book is an invitation to use what you can and eagerly seek more. The best music comes from struggle, augmentation, and collaboration. This book is a jumping-off point for more of those conversations, projects, and ciphers.

Further Reading

Katz, Mark. *Groove Music: The Art and Culture of the Hip-Hop DJ.* Oxford: Oxford University Press, 2012.

Pierznik, Christopher. *Hip-Hop Scholar: A Compendium of Rantings, Ravings, and Ruminations on Rap.* n.p.: CreateSpace Independent Publishing Platform, 2017.

Saucier, P. Khalil, and Tryon P. Woods. "Hip Hop Studies in Black." *Journal of Popular Music Studies* 26(2–3) (2014): 268–294.

Further Listening

Busta Rhymes. *The Coming.* Elektra Records, 1996.

The Fugees. *The Score.* Columbia Records, 1996.

Wyclef Jean. *The Carnival, Vol. 1.* Columbia Records, 1997.

Acknowledgments

My father, Rick Sciullo, is the greatest inspiration for anything I do. I thank him and my Italian ancestors, including, of course, Angelo and Jeanette Sciullo, for making me the thinker that I am and engaging me in my earliest years in rigorous thought, although often only about the virtues of the Pittsburgh Penguins' first line and chipped ham sandwiches. I received support from more people than I could ever possibly list. Thanks are due in large part to those who have worked on hip-hop and the law over the years: andré douglas pond cummings, Dr. Donald F. Tibbs, and the late great Pam Bridgewater. Other scholars have always pushed me to be better and supported my work across disciplines: Dr. Joe Bellon, Dr. Michael Lane Bruner, Dr. David Cheshier, Dr. Michael K. Davis, Dr. Patricia Davis, Atiba Ellis, Dr. Kevin Kuswa, Dr. Ronald W. Greene, Dr. Alessandra Raengo, and Caprice Roberts. It's not just the professors I've had and colleagues I've worked with who are due thanks but also all the people who have helped me along the way to better understand and appreciate music. All are intellectual forebearers to this project. Various scholarly institutions and communities have also been helpful: the Mid-Atlantic People of Color Conference, the West Virginia University College of Law, the Robert W. Woodruff Library at the Atlanta University Center, and the Osnabrück Summer Institute on the Cultural Study of Law. I have talked about hip-hop in the United States, England, and Germany. All the folks who have come to those talks or been involved in the various seminars have been helpful. Thanks also to friends from various places: Sara Baugh, Jeremy Broft, Harry Montoro, Luke Floyd, Robin Benson, and Amy Probasco. Thanks especially to Erin Hodgson, who has been a tremendous ally and all-around delight. She is a true friend, a champion of equality and critical thought, and someone I love genuinely. Caitlyn Moody and Meghan Roman wanted to be acknowledged for their role in making this book, and now their hilarity, friendship, and dogged determination to be awesome is so immortalized. Everyone mentioned here is great in their own right.

Introduction: The State of the Field of Hip-Hop Studies

This chapter will help define hip-hop and explain its broad significance for educators and students. Hip-hop is not obscure, and it is not something that only journalists and musicologists care to research. Most people, whether they like it or not, have come into contact with hip-hop. My argument is not that everyone should like or does like hip-hop but rather that hip-hop influences society nonetheless. One may not like the National Football League, but the conversation that its actions are causing about race and nationalism certainly influence U.S. culture. One doesn't have to have read *Harry Potter* to know that it is important and is shaping how a lot of people recreate (Quidditch, anyone?), among other things. Likewise, one might not understand vegetarianism or veganism and might actually think they're bad ideas, but that does not discount the way these movements influence marketing strategies of restaurants and food producers, nor does it deny how these ideas shape other service providers and entities such as wedding planners, conference venues, and hotels. Hip-hop likewise is out there and is shaping much of the world even if one doesn't feel particularly moved by hip-hop.

Even though this argument seems reasonable, it is difficult to convince people that something they don't do and may not have firsthand or even secondhand experience with affects them. For East Coast city types, it is often difficult to understand how the politics of the Midwest might affect them, yet every time a presidential election time rolls around, Iowa gets all the attention. Likewise, it might be difficult for Bavarians to understand how Berlin or Frankfurt affects them, but the financial and economic decisions made in those cities have far-reaching consequences across Germany and the whole of Europe. Culture works the same way. One need not be a member of any specific Latinx culture to hear the increased use of Spanish in the United States, and one's children do not need to be professional skateboarders or surfers to have an affinity for PacSun clothing stores. One of the most flummoxing issues of culture is that one can actively resist or even hate certain cultural forces, but those forces will still affect them. Think of the alt-right movements that are increasingly popular in the United States and Western Europe. In some way they are only relevant because of the things they hate and resist the most. Likewise, although I am not an avid listener of country music, I recognize that Darius Rucker, Dierks Bentley, and others are shaping popular music and that many people I interact with on a daily basis are listening to them. Hate hip-hop all you want, but this does not mean that it is going away or won't affect you, your family, or your coworkers. Culture is too fluid, too easily shared today.

Hip-hop is an important area of study. Educators are using hip-hop in classes at middle schools, high schools, colleges, and graduate and professional schools. Hip-hop provides examples of persuasion, argument, and analysis of a number of topics. It has visual and audible elements. So, it is not just that hip-hop can be analyzed like literature but that its music videos can be analyzed like television shows or movies, and its album covers can be analyzed like paintings. This makes hip-hop texts more than lyrics or beats, which makes hip-hop useful to many different disciplines and types of analysis.

Analogously, one might not care too much about classic rock, but this does not mean that the Beatles and the Rolling Stones are not important or that their music has not shaped how other artists make music or influenced how companies craft advertising campaigns. We don't have to like things to admit that they influence the world in which we live. In this way, it is important to recognize that although not everyone likes hip-hop—and indeed some people hate it—this does not mean that it is culturally insignificant. In fact, many hip-hop artists would argue that the evidence of haters is proof that the artists are doing important work and that this work is appreciated by many. As Soulja Boy raps, "Haters want to be me."

Hip-hop studies is a growing and dynamic field. Rather than simply the study of rap music, hip-hop studies encompasses a number of academic disciplines and considers a multitude of people, events, and texts. Simply put, hip-hop studies is a subsection of cultural studies that takes as its focus the complexity of hip-hop culture to better understand the culture on its own terms as well as apply hip-hop methodologies, theories, and lessons to other areas of culture. Its practitioners are in many disciplines with many different types of academic degrees and many with no academic degrees. Those people thinking critically about hip-hop are performers, scholars, and listeners.

Hip-hop is both an object of study—as with architecture in New York, women's rights movements in England, and the voting patterns of residents in U.S. southern cities—and a way to think about doing scholarly work in the ways that poststructuralism, realism, and ethnography may provide scholars, students, and activists with an orientation toward study. Hip-hop is such a large cultural phenomenon that there is a good chance scholars studying different parts of hip-hop may not even overlap in their work. A scholar focused on graffiti in New York may have little occasion to run into or come across a scholar working on French hip-hop in Paris. Likewise, a scholar invested in law and hip-hop might not do much work with English studies because both fields use different journals, different writing styles, and different conferences.

S. Craig Watkins argues that

> The growing array of hip-hop intellectuals is a spectacular indication of the movement's multifaceted demeanor and ceaseless energy. . . . What has emerged is a body of thinkers who articulate a wide range of ideas that, in their unique way, map out the contradictory currents, ideas, and worldview that percolate throughout the phenomenal world of hip hop. From spoken-word artists to academic scholars hip-hop intellectuals are translating the movement into a vast mix of critical commentary and artistic expression. The results both energize and expand the image and imagination of the hip-hop intelligentsia. (Watkins 2005, 234)

Watkins is excited by the diversity of contributors to and ideas in hip-hop studies. Writing in 2005, he recognizes the diversity of perspectives as a strength of the field, implicitly countering the argument often made against interdisciplinary fields that they are about too much and therefore about nothing. His understanding accepts the divisions in the field and embraces the importance of outsider knowledge so that it is not only professors who are valuable contributors in this space but also the emcees and spoken-word arts. Drawing on the tradition of phenomenology and ethnography, Watkins recognizes that intelligence and knowledge come from the ground up and not from the top down.

Monica Miller et al. argue that

> Hip Hop has become an astute public teacher to those who cared to listen to its weighty messages and learn from its many lessons. That is, Hip Hop necessitates anything but "easy" listening and passive consumption. Moreover, its messages of resistance, social awareness, personal consciousness, activism, pleasure and power, and community engagement have transcended its early days of locality in the Bronx and West Coast cities against the turmoil of post-industrialism. (Miller et al. 2014, 6)

This message importantly argues that locality is no longer a good way to think about hip-hop. That is, one need not be from New York to care about hip-hop studies. Miller and her coauthors also argue that hip-hop demands critical listening skills. Although many critics may deride hip-hop's lyrics, those critics often never consider the ways in which hip-hop self-polices its practitioners and critiques both practitioners and followers. Miller et al. also position hip-hop as a self-affirming art responding to critical postindustrialism ills such as rampant unemployment and systemic health care inequalities. If one is willing to listen, hip-hop has a lot to teach. That the *Journal of Hip Hop Studies* is now on its fifth volume is at least a partial indication that hip-hop studies is here to stay.

Hip-hop as an orientation to scholarship draws on the legacy of critical race theory. It seeks to understand oppression, control, racism, and the ways in which people of color often find themselves on the wrong side of law, public policy, and social relations. Critical race theory is a way of doing scholarship that was created by law professors in the 1980s who were troubled by the erasure of race from the legal curriculum. They recognized that there were racial disparities at every level of the criminal justice system and that the legal academy contained few minorities. They also realized that race was a defining characteristic of the United States, playing a prominent role in politics, law, and sociology as well as education, public health, and transportation infrastructure policy. Hip-hop studies scholars also share these views and direct their energy at addressing if not solving systemic inequality.

Hip-hop studies often takes for granted that racism is structural in the United States. It bears repeating: racism is structural in the United States. Oftentimes this shared assumption is a way that people express their downness with the cause. If one can agree that racism is structural, then one is probably on board for hip-hop as a way to think about racism. Hip-hop also appreciates performance and as such has allies in performance studies, communication, and theater. Hip-hop is not a staid art form that one experiences in a museum. It is something one experiences in concerts, at clubs, and in one's car. Mixtapes and CDs are traded, and the performance of those trades is itself interesting. You might be able to burn one CD of a particularly good artist or a new CD and trade it for several older CDs or less successful artists. The centrality of exchange also shapes hip-hop studies such that the remix, sampling, and sharing become central to understanding the circulation of ideas in hip-hop. One can understand a sample from a James Brown song, which evokes a different era and message; the African rhythm of a particular drum beat, which evokes a much longer musical heritage than late 1970s New York; or a diss track's relationship to another artist, song, or album. This intertextuality is also a key fixture of hip-hop. That is, hip-hop is often referencing other texts and historical periods.

This exchange underscores the sharing economy of hip-hop. Hip-hop studies is interested in the remix, or the way ideas are shared and changed from one rhetor to another. Hip-hop community members are concerned with sharing and the limits on sharing imposed by cultural norms and legal regimes. This sharing and the generative nature of the human condition are important for hip-hop scholars as they explore artistic creation and the importance of expression in one's sense of self.

Both perspectives, hip-hop as a thing to study and hip-hop as an orientation to studying, allow for critical inquiry. One can study the many aspects and actors of hip-hop as well as think about what hip-hop does to how we think about thinking. That is, hip-hop provides methodological and theoretical insights into many fields and issues. There are two ways of thinking about knowledge, broadly: epistemological and ontological. Epistemology is the study of knowledge, answering the question of how we know what we know. Ontology is the study of being, or how we are and what we are. Hip-hop is concerned with both. Hip-hop challenges institutional knowledges that deny slavery and systemic oppression. Hip-hop asks people to reconsider what they know about U.S. and world history and also understands that knowledge is passed down through people and that the present is structured by the struggles of the past. Likewise, hip-hop is deeply concerned with what it means to be in the world and not just what it means to be black, although many artists speak to this. Hip-hop asks who has agency and what people can do in this world to live fulfilling, meaningful lives when people, systems, and the menagerie of racism, classism, and other forms of invidious discrimination seem to rule the day. This book considers these perspectives and the ways in which both perspectives have influenced a number of different areas of culture and learning.

"Hip-hop" is a term used to mean many things. Traditionally, hip-hop has been understood to have four pillars: emceeing, DJing, graffiti, and break dancing. These pillars represent some of the foundational projects in which early hip-hoppers were engaged during the birth of hip-hop in the late 1970s in the Bronx, New York. Emceeing is the art of rapping, flowing, or engaging in a cypha. KRS-One, a hip-hop legend, draws a distinction between emceeing and rapping, arguing in the the song "Classic" that "Rappers spit rhymes that are mostly illegal / Emcees spit rhymes that uplift their people." This distinction, while perhaps seeming pedantic or trivial, is one that is still important in hip-hop, where artists are often criticized by hip-hop community members, scholars, and pundits for music that is violent or political.

Economic constraints on hip-hop artistry also shape the nature of hip-hop. Just as other industries have producers following trends, so too does hip-hop. Emceeing often takes second chair to party or club hip-hop, which has more commercial appeal to the masses. This division has resulted in artists decrying the commercialism of hip-hop and indeed caused some fracturing to this pillar. In many ways these tensions are unavoidable. Immortal Technique, in a spoken-word piece titled "The Poverty of Philosophy," says "But, I don't consider brothers a sellout if they move out of the ghetto. Poverty has nothing to do with our people. It's not in our culture to be poor." This understanding of the economic relationships between urbanites and people of color and the capitalist system that dominates the United States means that rather than shame those who have made money, become wealthy, and moved beyond impoverishment, hip-hop can accept earning money as a possibility that is quite in keeping with the history of success among people of color. The tension then between economic gain and amorphous ideas of authenticity or keeping it real or keeping it hood might in fact be artificial. Immortal Technique argues that earning money and bettering one's life is a natural outgrowth of hip-hop success. Technique's lyrics address one of the most common criticisms of hip-hop by those in the hip-hop community.

DJing is the process of playing records, now digital music files, and distorting, blending, and mashing up two different songs or tracks. Hip-hop DJing involves the active intervention of the DJ in the music, which would exclude from this notion of the DJ people who talk on the radio and introduce songs. DJing is often metonymically represented by the scratch, where a DJ would pull backward on a record to distort the sound of a record, creating a new sonic experience. A DJ clearly supports emceeing, as many DJs helped develop specific sounds that were understood to accompany certain emcees.

Hip-hop DJs and producers are and were stars in their own right. Certain artists produced sounds that labeled a track or even a party as their own: the trademark DJ Premier drop, the Timbaland baby sample, RZA's reliance on violins, and the transformer scratches of DJ Jazzy Jeff and Cash Money. While DJing began as a party routine, it soon resulted in DJs touring with emcees and then with DJs transitioning into production and working fewer parties. DJing, as a pillar of hip-hop, is understood to represent both party DJing and tour DJing as well as in-studio production.

Being a DJ was not simply about playing albums. DJs were certainly those people who changed songs on the radio, but they were also those people working with samplers, multiple tape decks, and turntables. It was DJs who often connected hip-hop to other forms of music through the crate-digging that allowed them to sample soul, disco, and R&B music. Today's top producers and DJs have an encyclopedic knowledge not only of what is playing now or in the last 10 years but also what has been popular for 50 or 60 years. This sort of knowledge has allowed hip-hop artists to continue to build on the tradition of black and urban music.

Graffiti encompasses the array of painting practices usually outdoors, where an artist tags (writes one's name), draws letters, symbols, or pictures using spray paint but also paint markers. Popular on billboards, bridges, and the sides of train cars, graffiti represents a foray into the world of art that draws anger from the establishment (property owners, government, etc.) while also encouraging serious artistic exploration. Graffiti is ubiquitous in modern culture and is often seen as a train passes by or in a bar's restroom. Perhaps less relevant to modern conceptions of hip-hop than it previously was, graffiti has influenced many of the artistic elements of hip-hop culture, from lettering style to album design to clothing. Graffiti-inspired works are on display in major international art museums (the Banksey exhibit at Amsterdam's Moco Museum, for example) and corporate advertising.

One can see graffiti-inspired t-shirts on youths across the world, a testament to its enduring effect. Graffiti helped emphasize that art was the domain of not just rich white people, which while historically inaccurate was an easy thing to think if one grew up in the shadows of the Museum of Modern Art or the Getty Museum. If you lived in Torrance, it might take you nearly a full day to use public transportation to get to the Getty. Art was not accessible in the 1980s and the 1990s like it seems to be today. Uber and Lyft provide much cheaper options than city taxis. The Internet seems to have virtually every artwork in museums scanned into it. Graffiti helped put art back in the hands of black populations. It is not that black people did not know art— African peoples have produced some of the most magnificent architectural and artistic forms in the history of humanity—but instead that museums were inaccessible. And whereas there are museums devoted to black art now, many of those museums were just being founded in the 1970s and 1980s. The African American Museum of the Arts in DeLand, Florida, was founded in 1994, and the Paul R. Jones Collection of African American Art wasn't founded in Newark, New Jersey, until 2004. Even if one could get to a museum there was no guarantee that any black artists would be on display, because museums have a troubled history of the way they have collected and shown minoritarian artifacts. Graffiti could be done with a thick marker (tagging) or a can or two of spray paint, much less expensive and time-consuming than multiple bus transfers and the price of admission to a museum. Graffiti remains popular as a people's form of art.

Break dancing originally consisted of performing complex dance maneuvers using one's entire body to make contact with the floor and spin around in a dizzying array of moves. Moves such as the windmill and the nickel literally propelled break dancing to the fore, although the worm seems to be the only remnant of break dancing that has made it into popular culture. Break-dancers, or b-boys (break dancing was predominantly practiced by boys and men, although women and girls quickly joined in participating), could be identified by carrying around a piece of cardboard such as a piece of an old appliance box (the cardboard is easier to spin on than the street) and a skull cap (skully or toboggan), which allowed head spins and other head moves to be more skillfully executed with a modicum of safety. Break dancing experienced a renaissance in the late 1990s through the early 2000s but since then has remained one of the smaller elements of hip-hop culture. Yet break dancing has influenced dancers around the world, and one often observes moves attributable to break dancing in the choreography of artists such as Usher, Beyoncé, and others.

There has been a resurgence of hip-hop dancing in fitness clubs and on television shows that highlight dance troupes. Break dancing remains popular in these cases, although it seems less important in many of the hip-hop communities across the United States. That is not to indicate that dance is less important. On the contrary, everything from the Humpty Dumpty to Dabbin' to the Crank That dance are popular across the country. So, even though break dancing seems less popular, other hip-hop dances have taken up the throne. Break dancing's fluid leg and arm movements are also obvious antecedents to these new dances, which often draw on some of the same movements and bodily comportments.

In the present day when people casually discuss hip-hop, they are most often referring to hip-hop music, which tends to emphasize emceeing. Rappers are the stars, whereas producers and DJs often exist in the background. In this book, "hip-hop" will be used both to mean hip-hop music and hip-hop culture as a whole. The most influential parts of hip-hop have been those involved in its musical attributes, as both lyrics and score have shaped not only ideas about culture and artistry but also politics, law, education, English, and other forms of intellectual inquiry, many of which are discussed in the proceeding chapters.

The recent literature on hip-hop is extensive. Hip-hop has its adherents across disciplines in the liberal arts as well as journalists, legal scholars, social workers, art and book critics, and many others. Hip-hop biographies and autobiographies are increasingly popular, represented by the works of and on artists such as Common, Wyclef Jean, DMX, Jay-Z, Eminem, and Dr. Dre, to name a few. Hip-hop might be usefully put to work in or for a number of areas, as indicated in the following chapters. Authors have written about hip-hop as a business, considering the billions of dollars it generates in album, concert, and merchandise sales as well as advertising and other related commerce. Hip-hop has also influenced businesses by suggesting new trends in marketing and product development as well as helping to describe new ways of thinking about working patterns such as hustling or grinding as ways of understanding worker practices.

In law, hip-hop finds itself implicated in contract and criminal law. Artists often have run-ins with the law and also critically engage law and government, critiquing it on grounds of racism and classism and along other critical lines. Hip-hop artists also impact the nature of free speech and artistic license. Some scholars have understood hip-hop's oppositional stance as a unique way into understanding law and also into understanding how students understand law. Perhaps hip-hop's greatest influence to cultural studies is that hip-hop, for better or worse, shapes the way some people understand the world.

In some ways, hip-hop's influence is unavoidable but also hard to decipher. There is no straight-line causal relationship between one artist and one development in this aspect of culture. Mechanistic views of culture hamper the complexities and exchanges of that culture, which are better understood as tapestries of interactions. One probably shouldn't wander around life trying to find hip-hop but instead should experience hip-hop in its entirety as a culturally pervasive form. In other words, one doesn't have to wander far. Whether student, scholar, journalist, activist, or professional, this book is intended to expose you to the ways hip-hop influences us all in various aspects of culture in the United States.

Hip-hop is often described as generational. That is to say, one might think of a hip-hop generation as people born between the mid-1960s and the early 1980s. While generational description can be fraught with difficulty, as generations are loose categories at best and lead to presumptions about identity at worst, one of the reasons why hip-hop is coming into its own as a subject of study is that people born during these time periods are now in positions of power as attorneys, doctors, professors, teachers, business leaders, and advocates. They would have come of age in the years when hip-hop was beginning and when it thrived in the 1990s and early 2000s, just as prior generations might be classified by their experience with the Jazz Age or the British Invasion.

M. K. Asante Jr., son of Afro-centric philosophy leading intellectual M. K. Asante, has also described the post–hip-hop generation as those people born from the mid-1980s through the 1990s. These community members are further distanced from and may be less familiar with racial struggles such as the civil rights movement, the war on drugs, and the Rodney King beating. Generally, the post–hip-hop generation is more comfortable with materialism and consumerism and desires less social consciousness in their music. They are also increasingly dissatisfied with the work of the hip-hop generation, refusing the hagiography of N.W.A. and Public Enemy and instead finding intellectual succor in Notorious BIG and Tupac Shakur. These changes are to be expected, of course, as everyone makes claims of knowing what the best music is or of the best way to study an era or artifact. The post–hip-hop generation adds important intellectual fire to hip-hop studies, ensuring that it remains relevant and self-reflexive.

For these reasons, hip-hop studies resembles other musical studies. The Jazz Age describes a period of time in the 1920s that was shaped by tremendous musical innovation and the rise of a certain type of affluence often associated with the Roaring Twenties, which is often described as overlapping with the Jazz Age. Likewise, LeRoi Jones (Amiri Baraka) described the history of African Americans in terms of music with a keen interest in the blues. In this way, Jones articulated complex cultural changes in time through music. Likewise, the punk and postpunk eras are used to describe certain periods of time that correspond to the British punk scene and the ways in which punk artists varied from those roots to usher in a wider aesthetic experience. One might quibble with ideas of generations, but mapping musical movements onto time periods has been an effective way of interrogating cultures throughout much of modernity.

Importantly, though, one should not conflate hip-hop studies with black or African American studies or urban studies. While the history of hip-hop can easily be told by reference to certain metropolitan areas, discussed below, hip-hop is neither solely a U.S. phenomenon nor only the province of urban denizens. Hip-hop artists exist across the world, and U.S.-based hip-hop is consumed in many places. Hip-hop happens in occupied Palestine, Standing Rock, and LaGrange, Georgia. White kids are the largest demographic group purchasing hip-hop and have been for years. You are increasingly likely to find hip-hop fans in the rural Midwest, where country music used to be an assumed favorite genre.

Of note although not central to this text is the regional variations of hip-hop. Artists are often fiercely territorial, something many readers will have a passing familiarity with respect to the 1990s East Coast verses West Coast feuds. It is no longer the case, and never really was, that hip-hop is monolithically represented by the West Coast, or Los Angeles, and the East Coast, or New York. While these areas still represent some of the largest areas for hip-hop artists, producers, and record labels, increasingly other regions of the country are developing their own talent and own sound. It is often possible to guess with some accuracy where an artist is from based on beat, vocal tone, pronunciation, and cadence.

Atlanta is now a hotbed of hip-hop activity represented by luminaries such as Ludacris and Outkast. The faster-moving beats and southern-inflected pronunciation of Atlanta artists is distinct from their New York or Houston counterparts. Trap music, a subset of hip-hop music, often focuses on life in the trap, understood as both a neighborhood and a house where drug-related and other criminal activity is frequent. Trap music grew out of the Atlanta hip-hop scene, represented by artists such as Gucci Mane and Yung Joc. Yung Joc raps "Meet me in the trap, it's goin' down," with a southern twang and Atlanta machismo. Once only listenable to during small concerts at the Masquerade or the Harlem Nights Ultra Lounge, Atlanta hip-hop now has a national following.

This legacy is now featured in television shows such as the series *Atlanta* that focuses not only on the city but also on the music industry. Helped by Donald Glover's international stardom from several other successful television and movie projects as well as his cult following as Childish Gambino, a welcome voice in the rap game in his own right, the show is exposing an ever larger audience to hip-hop. *Atlanta* provides a welcome antidote to *The Real Housewives of Atlanta,* which while certainly bringing viewers into contact with Atlanta and to a lesser degree hip-hop fails to galvanize the essence of Atlanta's urban denizens and musical proclivities.

Miami too is increasingly popular for hip-hop. Many artists there engage in predominantly party hip-hop, a reflection of southern Florida's diversity and propensity for opulent parties. DJ Khalid, Flo Rida ("Florida" divided into two words that evoke the notion of an emcee's flow and the idea of riding both as a musical act of following or being with a rhythm and the idea of representing one's self, crew, or posse), Trina, and Pitbull are readily identifiable artists who represent the Miami sound. Florida hip-hop combines the rhythms of the Caribbean world with Puerto Rican and Cuban artists while also drawing on the dance hall influences of contemporary Jamaican-based reggae. This hip-hop music is popular on the radio in Miami but also throughout the United States and the world and is often featured in clubs.

These distinct sounds and subject matters help unite hip-hop fans. This is important because it creates a community of listeners who have similar things to discuss: music, venues, artists, stylistic choices, etc. Fans can unite over these similar cultures and embrace their differences. In the same ways that sports fans unite around a region's teams, hip-hop fans often experience the same regional unity. This is one of hip-hop's community-building aspects, aside from shared artistic expression. While rivalries still exist, hip-hop has moved far from the East Coast–West Coast rivalries of the 1990s and the New York borough rivalries of the 2000s. One might hesitate to state it, but one can in fact now like Houston rap and New York rap. Even with differences, hip-hop allows conversations about similar subject matters and unity in the necessary pursuit of having a good time.

But, it is not that hip-hop only grows around the biggest U.S. cities and regions such as Hampton Roads, Virginia; St. Louis, Missouri; and Cleveland, Ohio. To be sure, hip-hop originated in inner cities in the northeast but is now a nationwide phenomenon, one that is increasingly relevant internationally. Not only do rappers and producers incorporate international musical influences in their work, but they also appear more often internationally. Other countries and regions are also developing vibrant hip-hop scenes, including Toronto, Canada; London, England; Cairo, Egypt; and Paris, France. In cosmopolitan world cities, one is as likely to hear U.S. artists as they are to hear local artists, and increasingly international artists are gaining air time in the United States. Artists such as Drake and Kardinal Offishall, both from Toronto, are some of the most popular artists of the last several years. In the early and mid-2000s it was impossible to not hear a Kardinal Offishall song in clubs, and Drake has become one of the most successful rappers at present.

While hip-hop has often found success in cities with significant populations of people of color, hip-hop also has roots in other areas outside of large cities. Appealing to different audiences has a long tradition in black music, from the blues and jazz through Ray Charles and Aaron Neville's forays into a more country-style sound. Hip-hop is well positioned in nonurban spaces with artists such as Cowboy Troy, more a country artist than a hip-hop artist, as well as Bubba Sparxx, Yelawolf, and Nelly representing a distinctly country-influenced hip-hop style. But these artists and collaborations between country and hip-hop artists have also met with their fair share of criticism. Some of this has been a response to some less than stellar songs, and other criticism has been directed at individual artists and the messages of the songs. Brad Paisley and LL Cool J's collaboration on "Accidental Racist" drew much criticism as both a song and a message. The song blended country and hip-hop styles in an attempt to address issues of southern blame and pride as well as the country's racial problems, and also represents an attempt to bridge the gap between country and hip-hop music.

No matter where one calls home, hip-hop's pervasive influence is all around. From city to country, from the United States and beyond, hip-hop has affected the way we all listen to music, relate to each other, and consume media and other products and services. One needn't be a fan of hip-hop or be black or from New York to experience hip-hop's influence. Tommy Hilfiger clothing and Beyoncé's marriage to hip-hop mogul Jay-Z still dominates gossip blogs and magazines. Artists such as Common have been to the White House, and classes on hip-hop are taught around the country at colleges and universities. MTV once seemed more influenced by hip-hop than any other music form; examples include DJ Scribble's ubiquitous spring break performances and Sway, MTV's most recognizable personality. Do you like Vitamin Water? Queens-born 50 Cent propelled the Glaceau-made vitamin water product to popularity. Are you a St. John's University alum? You and J. Cole should enjoy a beverage at the next tailgate party. Do you enjoy a flattering Marc Ecko bag, coat, or watch or reading *Complex* magazine? Ecko may be the preeminent hip-hop–influenced designer with a billion-dollar lifestyle company. The point is, of course, that hip-hop is all around us whether we enjoy the music or not.

In many respects, we should expect hip-hop to influence us. Music always has. Plato bans the flute in Book Three of *The Republic* and not the lyre because the flute represents a level of musicality so rapturous to the tripartite conception of the soul that it couldn't possibly be maintained in the city. The music was too distracting, too influential. But the lyre, with its one string, was manageable. People could get on with life. So, this early representation of music's power serves as a good example of the way music can dramatically shape society. Of course, the history of American music, from slave spirituals to blues and from jazz to rock and roll, reggae, and British punk, have all shaped the United States and other countries. Hip-hop is in some ways just another example, yet it is our most recent example of a genre with such broad influence. Music has always influenced politics, other art forms, business marketing strategies, educators, and writers. This book takes for granted that music can influence other aspects of culture and that hip-hop is a popular form of music that also influences culture. Rather than spend half of the text defending hip-hip from its critics, this book assumes that like all musical styles and like all musical artists, hip-hop and hip-hop artists are flawed.

That is not to say that hip-hop is always riveting social critique. It does not have to be, just as we do not expect every novel and every painting to pose a direct challenge to the ills of the world. However, hip-hop in some ways is always political. As Bryan McCann has articulated, hip-hop is a way to express oneself and a way to orient oneself toward the world that challenges norms. So, even where there might be what is regarded as a dance track or a club hit, that music too is political because it represents a sonic expression of joy that was historically prohibited. In this sense, hip-hop often represents the mainstreaming of musical expression once banned by slave owners. Slaves were prohibited from talking, dancing, and singing on many planta-tions in the United States, and every time slaves broke those rules they were engaged in a politically powerful act of resistance. Slave owners feared the empowering force of artistic expression and the potential unifying force that this expression could have for slaves. The production value may be different now, but hip-hop often operates in the same register.

Hip-hop has been assailed for years as violent, materialistic, and misogy-nistic. To be sure, some artists are guilty of these beliefs and of promoting them in their music. But hip-hop promises teaching and learning opportuni-ties that can benefit from serious engagement. The criticism of hip-hip might rightfully be traced to former Secretary of Commonwealth for Pennsylvania C. Delores Tucker, who waged a prolonged battle against gangsta rap, a sub-genre of hip-hop prominent in the early to mid-1990s. Tucker directed most of her anger against Tupac Shakur, perhaps the most prominent West Coast rapper ever. Tupac, the godson of Assata Shakur, composed and performed lyrics rich with metaphor and wordplay that promoted, contrary to Tucker's claims, a prowomanist message that resonated with the importance of the women in his life, such as Leila Steinberg. Artists such as Common and Talib Kweli have written songs about the value of women in their lives and the importance of uplifting women. Female emcees such as MC Lyte and Queen Latifah have consistently promoted feminist messages, and even those female artists with raunchy lyrics such as Lil' Kim and Foxy Brown have argued that their music is about the freedom of women to express themselves even if that expression isn't favored by those in the mainstream, a mainstream that is often male, Anglo, and moneyed.

Recently, Jay-Z's "The Story of O.J." contained a line that caused many to worry over his potential anti-Semitism. He rapped about how having good credit mattered, stating "You ever wonder why Jewish people own all the property in America? This how they did it." He responded that the line was about exaggerated racism, just as the video and song address the racism experienced by black people. The music video contains a cartoon representation of a black person with the racist dark skin and large lips prominent in depictions of black people in the first half of the 20th century. Jay-Z's claim that he is critiquing these sorts of argumentation make sense in the context of the song and the music video, but hip-hop is no stranger to these sorts of statements, particularly discrimination against homosexuals, which is best exemplified by the problematic way homosexuality and homophobia are addressed in certain reggae music. The term "batty boy," a slur against gay men, features prominently in songs by MF Doom ("Batty Boyz"), Mega Banton ("Shot a Batty Bow"), Beenie Man ("Victory [Chi Chi Man Fi Dead]"), and Capleton ("Battyman Fi Get Boom"). "Chi chi man" is another slur against homosexual men used in certain reggae and hip-hop lyrics. Unfortunately, reggae and hip-hop have done a poor job addressing homophobia, something that any hip-hop listener must be willing to critique.

However, hip-hop's most objectionable songs and personas do not stand in for its best. Just as one might decry certain country music artists or songs, Beatles copycats, or emo/punk music, so too can we decry hip-hop for its worst practitioners. But such stereotyping is lazy and a poor excuse to not engage this art form. Never are people simplified to their best or worst acts. No idea or political party can only be understood through its excesses. Before condemning hip-hop, think about it in its many manifestations. Then, if one feels it necessary, make a pronouncement on par with Nas's notion that hip-hop is dead.

Each of the following chapters addresses hip-hop in or about different areas of culture. By culture, I mean the manifestations of human collective achievement. While we can discuss hip-hop culture or subculture, this book is not just about hip-hop; it is about hip-hop in other realms of culture, hip-hop in life. This approach is intended to provoke an appreciation for hip-hop's relationship to what might be otherwise understood as autonomous spheres of culture. Some of the applications are easier than others, often as a result of the tremendous work of scholars to apply hip-hop to their work or put their interests and training to work on hip-hop (law and education). Others are more difficult because scholars and professionals have less of a record doing this work (business). What this means, though, and what this book argues is that hip-hop can be fruitfully studied in a number of areas by many scholars and practitioners even though they may not have previously thought about pursuing these avenues.

Although this book is written with a firm founding in the scholarship on hip-hop, one should not assume that hip-hop is only an esoteric academic subject. Professionals in a variety of fields might find hip-hop rewarding as well. Imagine working with patients who feel more at ease when they are able to listen to the music they enjoy or when their doctor can have a comment or two about a new album. Social workers and psychologists who are able to use music as therapy or as a metaphor for clients' problems might make it easier for clients to discuss their troubles. It is much easier to discuss one's troubles if one doesn't have to come out and announce them at the first meeting. Likewise, managers and leaders will need to understand that millennials bring new cultural references and musical tastes to the workplace. And it does not matter if one works in a law office or a clothing store. Business experts in places ranging from the *Harvard Business Review* to the many work and management blogs across the Internet have argued that generational shifts have radically changed the workplace. No one is suggesting that a senior partner in an accounting firm be able to recite the newest J. Cole single, but having an appreciation for basic concepts such as "hustle," "the come up," and "grindin'" might help managers and leaders understand why younger workers act the way they do and what motivates them.

Hip-hop is also a meditation of difficult times. It is an outlet for people in dire straits. One of the earliest and most popular hip-hop acts, Grandmaster Flash and the Furious Five, rapped in "The Message" that "Sometimes it makes me wonder / How I keep from goin' under." This early hip-hop song sounded an important message that would be retold time and time again. In desperate times, impoverished and neglected neighborhoods were at a tipping point. There were few options available. People felt limited in their ability to succeed and their ability to challenge the systems that seemed to disenfranchise them. Grandmaster Flash spoke to a generation of people in the 1980s who had to navigate the beginning of aggressive policing, the reduction of social services, and the crack epidemic. This work matters now.

Further Reading

Asante, M. K., Jr. *It's Bigger Than Hip Hop: The Rise of the Post–Hip-Hop Generation.* Basingstoke, UK: Macmillan, 2008.

Cepeda, Raquel. *"And It Don't Stop": The Best American Hip Hop Journalism of the Last 25 Years.* London: Faber and Faber, 2004.

Chang, Jeff. *Can't Stop, Won't Stop: A History of the Hip-Hop Generation.* London: Picador, 2005.

George, Nelson. *Hip Hop America.* New York: Penguin, 1998.

Miller, Monica, et al. "The Hip in Hip Hop: Toward a Discipline of Hip Hop Studies." *Journal of Hip Hop Studies* 1(1) 2014: 6–12.

Price, Emmett George. *Hip Hop Culture.* Santa Barbara, CA: ABC-CLIO, 2006.

Schloss, Joseph G. *Making Beats: The Art of Sample-Based Hip-Hop.* Middletown, CT: Wesleyan University Press, 2004.

Watkins, S. Craig. *Hip Hop Matters: Politics, Pop Culture, and the Struggle for the Soul of a Movement.* Boston, MA: Beacon, 2005.

Further Listening

Common. "I Used to Love H.E.R.," on *Resurrection*. Relativity, 1994.
Kanye West, Nas, KRS-One, and Rakim. "Classic (Better Than I Ever Been DJ Premier Remix)." Nike, 2007.
KRS-One and Marley Marl. "I Was There," on *Hip Hop Lives*. Koch, 2007.
Wyclef. "Hip Hop," on *April Showers*. Carnival, 2013.
Wyclef Jean. "Industry," on *The Preacher's Son*. J Records, 2003.

CHAPTER ONE

Legal Education and Hip-Hop

One of the most highly developed bodies of literature concerns hip-hop and the law. When discussing hip-hop and the law, one is considering both the ways that hip-hop and hip-hop artists interact with the law across its various types (criminal, constitutional, family, First Amendment, etc.), as well as the ways in which hip-hop may provide insights into law, government, and public policy. Both are discussed in this chapter. Still met with skepticism, often as a result of concern about law school curricula and bar passage rates, hip-hop and the law is an interesting area of study. One is unlikely to find the word "hip-hop" on a bar exam, but this does not mean that hip-hop doesn't provide opportunities for critical thinking, logical reasoning, and hypothesis testing. Hip-hop's vast cultural significance means that it can be analyzed in a number of law school classes, just as one might consider sports law or family law as requiring not a knowledge of a discrete subsection of law but rather an understanding of law broadly across a number of different specialties that reveal the complexities of human interaction.

Hip-hop's own interdisciplinary focus helps students understand law's complex ideas and also compliments law's theorizing of critical race theory and intersectionality. This is why hip-hop and law scholars come from not only legal backgrounds but also sociology, history, communication, rhetorical studies, and English studies. These cognate fields have provided additional resources for lawyers and legal scholars for centuries. Because hip-hop is a business, a musical form, a writing and speaking project, a community-building forum, etc., it provides ample ideas and ways to think about ideas for legal scholars, even those not in a law school or with a law degree. That interdisciplinary nature mirrors the ways in which hip-hop has developed with graffiti artists becoming DJs, such as DJ Kay Slay, and DJs becoming emcees, such as Ludacris.

Research on hip-hop and the law has been a quickly growing subdiscipline of law and legal studies as well as hip-hop studies. This area of work was born out of Paul Butler's monumental work "A Hip-Hop Theory of Punishment," published in the *Stanford Law Review* in 2004. Then a professor of law at George Washington University, Butler laid the groundwork for considering how hip-hop could influence legal thinking. He followed up this article with *Let's Get Free: A Hip-Hop Theory of Justice* in 2009. Butler's bona fides as a professor at a top law school, with publication in a top law review, years of experience as a prosecutor, and a law degree from Harvard Law School encouraged scholars to take hip-hop and the law seriously.

Butler was not the only legal scholar to work on hip-hop issues. Shortly after this work, legal scholars who worked predominantly in entertainment law and criminal law began to incorporate hip-hop into their writing. The constraints on what counts as scholarship, though, meant that many scholars had to wait until they had been promoted before venturing into areas that the traditional law school professional community viewed with suspicion. This was not unique to law scholarship. Academic study still maintains a good amount of rigidity, so the work that early legal scholars were doing on hip-hop did not translate well into a world that evaluated research on the parol evidence rule or the finer points of collateral estoppel.

Nonetheless, I and other scholars such as Pamela Bridgewater, andré douglas pond cummings, Akilah Folami, and Donald F. Tibbs engaged in an extensive publishing and presenting campaign in law reviews and at conferences across the world, spreading the interest in hip-hop and law. Both Folami and I demonstrated the ways in which this scholarship could be and was indeed theoretically rich, working through ideas from Jürgen Habermas, Kenneth Burke, Gilles Deleuze, and Felix Guattari in the context of hip-hop scholarship. This work, important because hip-hop and law work was unfairly viewed as not rigorous, helped introduce scholars to the complexities of hip-hop and its utility as an analytical lens.

In 2009, the West Virginia University College of Law hosted "The Evolution of Street Knowledge: Hip-Hop's Influence on Law and Culture." The conference brought together leading thinkers and was keynoted by Dr. Cornel West, one of the leading black public intellectuals of the last 30 years, and Talib Kweli, a Brooklyn-based socially conscious rap artist. Lasting for two days, the conference involved lively discussions with law professors, scholars in related disciplines, community members, and law and graduate students. This conference gave rise to the publication *Hip Hop and the Law* in 2015. The scholars at Street Knowledge would go on to present at conferences around the world. The conference also helped ensure that a community of scholars had outlets for discussing their work. As an online extension of the conference, *Hip Hop and the Law* became participants' go-to blog for sharing cutting-edge ideas about hip-hop and law.

Hip Hop and the Law also considers the ways in which people write, read, and understand law in their social positions, a process sometimes described as "coming to the law." This bottom-up critique of law can help lawyers and lawyers-to-be understand how their clients understand law. In the same ways that television, radio, movies, and other media shape knowledge about ideas and people, hip-hop shapes the ways people understand law, for better or worse. One need not make a normative claim about this process, but surely one must recognize that music influences perceptions of the world.

This expanded view of hip-hop and law led Kim Chanbonpin, a professor of law at John Marshall Law School (Chicago), to publish "Legal Writing, the Remix: Plagiarism and Hip Hop Ethics" in the *Mercer Law Review* in 2012. Chanbonpin's argument is that hip-hop is an important teaching tool in the legal classroom. She bases that argument on hip-hop's important commentaries of authenticity, evidence, argument, and credibility, to name a few. Because students often come to law school with more experience in hip-hop than with William Blackstone or David Hume, hip-hop can serve as a bridge to help students understand the mechanistic process of legal writing and rule making. Chanbonpin's article helped highlight hip-hop as a teaching tool, as not only a theoretical intervention but also a pedagogical one.

In 2015, Pamela Bridgewater (Washington College of Law at American University), andré douglas pond cummings (Indiana Tech Law School), and Donald F. Tibbs (Drexel Law School) published *Hip Hop and the Law,* an edited collection that reprinted existing scholarship and featured new work by legal scholars from around the world. This book helped display the breadth of law and hip-hop work with articles addressing not only criminal and contract law but also real property, gender, race, mass incarceration, corporate law, critical race theory, and sociology. The book galvanized years of scholarship and helped add further legitimacy to the field.

Additional work on hip-hop will continue to follow this pattern. Legal scholars will publish essays, books, and blogs devoted to the subject. What might happen soon is that we begin to have more hip-hop artists take part directly in legal scholarship. We will continue to have hip-hop lyrics cited in relevant court cases and other legal documents. Such work, while troubling to many traditional practitioners and scholars, will reflect the continued importance of hip-hop to how we all think about law.

As an object of study, hip-hop might have its clearest involvement in law with the legal troubles of De La Soul and Biz Markie. Both situations involved sampling, or the practice of using another song in one's own song. De La Soul was subject to a $1.7 million settlement for using a few seconds of a Turtles' song. Sampling is significant in hip-hop, as hip-hop builds on previous styles of music, yet using other people's work can be difficult if one does not ask permission. The Biz Markie situation involved the record company attempting to get clearance for a sample, which was denied by the original artist,

Gilbert O'Sullivan. The record label, Warner Brothers, used the sample anyway. A legal conflagration ensued whereby Judge Kevin Duffy found Biz Markie guilty of infringing on O'Sullivan's copyright and barred Warner Brothers from selling the album and the single. The matter was also referred to criminal court for Biz Markie's alleged theft, although he was never prosecuted. The case revolutionized sampling, making it an intensely business activity. The process of getting clearances became much more complicated and more important, as significant monetary damages were at stake. Biz Markie would later release the album *All Samples Cleared!* that made fun of his courtroom drama while also highlighting in the liner notes that he had meticulously cleared all samples. The album cover also featured Biz playing judge and defendant, a visual reference to the court case that stood in for his lack of mentioning the case in the album itself.

Hip-hop artists also made trenchant critics of law. Many were critical of policing practices and argued that police discriminated not just against hip-hop artists but also against black and brown people across the United States. As a result, jails were overcrowded from discriminatory policing practices, and black families were decimated by harsh sentencing, the war on drugs, and racial profiling. N.W.A's 1988 hit "Fuck Tha Police" became a street anthem, tapping the anger of young black men and women sick of unfair policing. KRS-One's "Sound of Da Police" followed up on this successful model of criticizing the police in 1993. This model also served as the foundation for hip-hop songs that weren't simply critical of but openly violent toward police, which of course inspired criticism from law enforcement agents and organizations as well as other advocacy groups. While one might reasonably criticize any advocacy of violence, the hip-hop artists who advocated violence against police were on firm theoretical footing with respect to how the oppressed could challenge the violence they perceived by counteracting with equally dramatic violence.

So, Ice T, who ironically would go on to play a police officer on the long-running NBC drama *Law & Order: SVU,* released "Cop Killer" in 1992. President George H. W. Bush and Vice President Dan Quayle were vocal in their criticism of the song, which contained lines such as "I'm 'bout to bust some shots off . . . to dust some cops off." In 2000 dead prez released "Cop Shot" in which the duo rapped "Keep shooting. . . . We will shoot back." These lyrics illustrate the intense anger and frustration felt by people of color who no longer, if they ever did, feel safe when interacting with police. It would be easy to write off these lyrics as violent, ill-conceived, and dangerous, yet this does not mean that they weren't created in response to the pervasive problems of police brutality, racial profiling, and discriminatory sentencing practices. That is, the problems that these lyrics address are real and worthy of engagement.

Hip-hop has also taken on the legal process with Lauryn Hill's "Mystery of Inequity" and Common's "Testify," both representative of gripping legal dramas. Hill's critique of the court system is replete with metaphor and word play. She raps "Swearing by The Bible blatantly blasphemous. . . . Publicly perpetrating that In God We Trust." This critique resonates as a moralistic quandary, as the justice system seemingly abides by or affiliates with a notion of Christian morality yet engages in systematic inequality that undermines the utility of those notions. Furthermore, the scriptological beginning calls into question the authenticity of the written word (court briefs, lawyer memos, jail transfer paperwork, etc.). In so doing, Hill implicates ideas about statutory and contract construction that rely on the written word as paramount in construction (e.g., the parol evidence rule). Common tells the story of a courtroom duped by a female perpetrator highlighting the imperfections in the legal system while also casting doubt on the notion of black male criminality. Both the male accused of the crime and his romantic partner are black. The prosecutor is also black—played by Steve Harris, who in NBC's *The Practice* played a defense attorney—calling to mind the fluidity of accused and accuser, defense attorney and prosecutor. Common, in the music video, relies on the viewer invoking other cultural knowledge to contextualize his critique; this does not diminish the value of the criticism but instead indicates just how important cultural knowledge is to certain types of hip-hop. So, Common then understands law in society rather than law apart from society and respects his audience enough to set up a referential system that enables deeper reflection and the placing of hip-hop's critique of law in its broader context.

Relatedly, hip-hop has also taken on electoral politics, with artists writing songs both in support of and opposed to various elected officials. Law and politics are intimately intertwined, to which anyone familiar with the last several presidential election cycles in the United States can attest. While not strictly legal in nature, these songs address laws and policies commonly discussed in law classrooms, courtrooms, and graduate seminars. Perhaps not surprisingly, many hip-hop artists were fiercely critical of President George W. Bush and fiercely supportive of President Barack Obama. In the song "Why," Jadakiss rapped "Why did Bush knock down the towers?"—making a powerful suggestion that Bush and his policies were potentially responsible for the September 11, 2001, attack on the World Trade Center. This attack on Bush was not the only one. In 2002 in "The Proud," Talib Kweli criticized both the president and vice president in a larger verse about questionable government policies.

The election of Obama as president brought about tremendous jubilation from hip-hop artists. They released a litany of songs. Young Jeezy and Nas's "My President" was one of the most popular. Jeezy raps "Obama for mankind . . . let the man shine." And will.i.am raps "Yes we can to justice and equality. . . . Yes we can." This approbation earned air time on popular and urban radio stations as well as countless streaming listens and YouTube video watches. Obama, who settled in Chicago as an adult and is biracial, became the first nonwhite president of the United States. He looked like, at least based on color, many hip-hop artists and was geographically marked as caring about urban issues and people because he came from a racially diverse northern city.

In some ways this ought not be surprising. Hip-hop artists, like everyone else, have opinions on law. What makes hip-hop so interesting as a strategy for legal engagement is that it brings minoritarian perspectives to law in ways that they haven't been brought before. Hip-hop not only includes voices of color and impoverished voices but also brings them to the forefront without the master's tools. Hip-hop is categorically different from a pro se pleading. Hip-hop is not a brief or public statement by the local legal aid society or the public defender's office. Rather than assume that these voices can only matter in formal legal proceedings and documents, hip-hop emboldens communication on legal matters in other ways, utilizing the full expanse of multimedia. This made legal commentary easier for people who already felt locked out of the courthouse by personnel and procedures that seemed both confusing and positioned against them.

Seattle-based rapper Macklemore argued that "No law's gonna change us, we have to change us" in a song about same-sex marriage that provides a welcome response to rampant homophobia in hip-hop. The line is also an important critique of law. Law is a social construct, something many students learn in political science classes and law school, but a social construct that is resistant to challenges and one that changes slowly. While it is easy to externalize progress and hope that it comes from changes to laws, Macklemore argued that what we need to do is change how we think about homosexuality. This refocused criticism on individuals and how they uphold the problematic actions and ideas that allow horrible laws to be in place. For example, historically the only way substantial changes were made to check antiblackness was a shift in how the population viewed black people. The Reconstruction Amendments, *Brown v. Board of Education,* and the Voting Rights Act, though not silver bullets, happened in part because people were rethinking their relationship to blackness and what it meant to live in a world where they could no longer rationalize certain legal discriminations against people of color.

Hip-hop in some ways is fundamentally about access to the social world. In law, this often means that hip-hop is a way to communicate about legal issues in a world where not everyone can afford a lawyer or knows how to communicate one's case even with a lawyer. It means engaging in hip-hop because one does not know how to make an application to the court as well as any number of other issues. It means reclaiming one's neighborhood by using graffiti to challenge the bourgeois advertising of retailers who are all too happy to advertise in a neighborhood but are reticent to hire anyone from the same neighborhood. While music seems almost easy to understand as legal critique, it is also the other elements of hip-hop that present a challenge to legal norms.

An interesting new development in hip-hop and law work is the use of hip-hop lyrics as evidence. While artists likely assume that art, while it may reflect the artist's reality, is a creative expression more so than a statement of fact, courts are beginning to use hip-hop lyrics as evidence of crime. The scenario plays out like this: a hip-hop artist describes some criminal event or mocks someone who is dead or injured, and those lyrics are used to prove that the artist is guilty of the crime. Movies and advertisements also do these things, but no one seems likely to charge Michael Bey with inciting a robot revolt. Prosecutors are also using lyrics as evidence of supporting criminal activities and organizations. If an artist raps about the glories of being a Blood or a Crip, two of the most prominent gangs in the United States, then those lyrics could be used to charge the artist with supporting a criminal organization. This is the story of San Diego–based rapper Brandon Duncan. This conundrum puts criminal law, evidence law, and freedom of speech on trial and could implicate hundreds of hip-hop artists. Legal scholars such as Donald J. Tibbs have been discussing this issue, but more work is still to be done.

Of course, criticism of hip-hop and the law comes from both inside and outside the legal academy. It is not simply that the law work isn't legal enough but also that hip-hop and the law represent an institutionalization of hip-hop in an education system that has often been shown to be racist, sexist, classist, and more. Some critics have argued that hip-hop was and is about the streets but not about the brick-lined walkways of this country's law schools. These critics had a point. The ethos of resistance that many hip-hop community members fostered had an awkward fit in the hallowed halls of law schools. It was, after all, these law schools that were training future prosecutors to incarcerate people of color, inner-city residents, and hip-hop artists. This irony, though, was an opportunity for hip-hop and the law to create more compassionate-thinking attorneys and activists. While hip-hop legal scholars might have preferred to abolish prisons or at least usher in new sentencing guidelines and end imprisonment for low-level drug offenses, the more modest goals of these scholars was to help students think more clearly about race and justice in a changing world. That involved a bit of institutionalization, but it also provided students an opportunity to think about law and culture in ways that they might not have, which could lead and no doubt has led to a better understanding of how people think about law, police, and justice.

Further Reading

Bridgewater, Pamela, andré douglas pond cummings, and Donald F. Tibbs, eds. *Hip Hop and the Law*. Durham, NC: Carolina Academic Press, 2015.

Butler, Paul. *Let's Get Free: A Hip-Hop Theory of Justice.* New York: New Press, 2009.

Butler, Paul. "Much Respect: Toward a Hip-Hop Theory of Punishment." *Stanford Law Review* 56 (2004): 983–1016.

Chanbonpin, Kim. "Legal Writing, the Remix: Plagiarism and Hip Hop Ethics." *Mercer Law Review* 63 (2012): 597–638.

Further Listening

Common. "Testify," on *Be.* GOOD Music, 2005.

dead prez. "Cop Shot." Raptivism Records, 2000.

Jadakiss. "Why," on *Kiss of Death.* Ruff Ryders, 2004.

Snoop Doggy Dogg. "Murder Was the Case," on *Doggystyle.* Death Row, 1993.

CHAPTER TWO

Educational Studies and Hip-Hop

Educational studies demands an increased focus on diversity, as student bodies are increasingly diverse along race, class, gender, national origin, and age lines. This has allowed hip-hop, with its emphasis on the remix, to address an increasingly fragmented and culturally rich educational environment and thus has allowed educators to push the boundaries of curriculum instruction and policy studies.

One of the most important issues to consider when thinking about how all people learn is that school-age children will often be influenced by hip-hop. This means that teachers will need to reconsider what their students like and know. Bob Dylan, the Rolling Stones, Marvin Gaye, and even Britney Spears will not cut it as references. Teachers will need to expand how they think about music and culture in order to meet students at their level. This does not necessarily mean moving away from Homer or F. Scott Fitzgerald, but it might mean reading Tupac's poetry in English class, using math examples that reference total units (of CDs or vinyl albums) pressed instead of refrigerators, and discussing in political science classes the Black Lives Matter movement as much as the civil rights movement. It is not that one is necessarily better but rather that changing a teacher's perspective can help students gain some perspective.

Education studies has long struggled with change. It can be difficult to rethink how education is delivered. Of course, theorists such as Paulo Freire and Henry Giroux have shaped how we now teach, but changes have also occurred relative to models of teaching—from lectures to group work to flipping the classroom. Hip-hop supports alternative styles of learning, values participation and collaboration, and recognizes that some of the best material comes from the bottom up and not from the top down. As we rethink teaching, we will hopefully do away with the idea that the teacher always knows more, something Freire taught us years ago, but disturbingly few changes have been made in many classrooms across the United States. Teachers of all grades continually talk down to and demean students as if they brought nothing to the educational experience. Hip-hop should teach a corrective to this.

Although *Brown v. Board of Education* is more than 65 years old, the integration of schools was no easy process. This was true not only in the U.S. South but also in the mid-Atlantic and the North. Many school systems ignored the U.S. Supreme Court or reinforced de facto segregation by housing, busing, and other policies that kept black and white people separated even though schools were supposed to be integrated. Today's urban centers are still dealing with these changes, and there are many schools that are de facto segregated as a result of funding decisions and other public policy issues advanced as race-neutral. Hip-hop asks educators to think about what people are learning, who is learning, and who is teaching. Rather than accept education as a public good, some hip-hop artists argued that education is actively harming students of color because it teaches irrelevance and a lack of self-worth.

Christopher Emdin frames the discussion this way in *Urban Science Education for the Hip-Hop Generation:*

> Imagine if you could spend every second of the next three years in an institution that values who you are, embraces where you come from, and teaches what has been described as the most challenging subject matter in a way that is engaging, respectful of your culture, and aligned to the way that you see the world. The feelings that would be generated from that experience would be able to propel you into new possibilities for your future. You might be convinced that what has been previously presented as challenging, is really not anything out of your intellectual reach. Your confidence would grow, your faith in your academic abilities would develop, and over time, you would begin to see that you have the tools to be successful at whatever task is set in front of you. (Emdin 2010, xi)

This is the world that many people of color are not experiencing. They do not experience an education system that affirms them or recognizes their role in learning. Teachers often do not look like them and have little faith in their ability. The material is not engaging, and many teachers simply do not care if it is. That is an uneducational space where curriculum and tradition take precedence over students. That is a space where the future seems bleak and where trying does not seem to promise any real benefit.

Educational studies also faces a crisis. Not everyone is comfortable discussing hip-hop, hearing it on a student's phone, or even analyzing the complex lyrics, with their allusions and metaphors. It can be uncomfortable for teachers to engage texts with which they are unfamiliar, but of course teachers have been doing this forever. Some English teachers focused more on composition than literature during their college training. Indeed, many focused on British literature and not American literature, poetry and not prose. One's U.S. history teacher may actually have specialized in European history, and one's softball coach may actually have played golf. So, teachers, who have proven to be tremendously adaptable and responsive to their student populations, should fear not. Everyone can work with hip-hop. A little summer preparation or reading and listening over winter break should be more than enough. Students also appreciate effort, so educators can admit that they are not experts or participants in hip-hop culture and still use hip-hop to teach.

Educators might also use hip-hop as a way to flip the classroom in the educational parlance of the day. Inviting a student up to discuss why a certain song illustrates a point in history, sociology, or business can help students take charge of their learning. This can get students comfortable with teaching and with making presentations. It also emphasizes that students have knowledge and can share that knowledge. That is, the teacher isn't the only one who has intelligent things to say. Further, allowing students to discuss popular culture texts in an academic setting can help demystify the academic process and encourage students to put theories they learn in the classroom to work in their lives.

Why use hip-hop texts besides meeting students at their level? Hip-hop songs often last between three and six minutes, making them ideal for assignments and course plans designed to last one course period. The verse structure of many songs also makes them ripe for chunking. Chunking is the selection of small pieces of a larger text to make a text easier to work with. A verse can be a chunk. Because songs often have several verses, groups might also be assigned a verse each. These factors make hip-hop ideal for classroom use.

KRS-One's "Hip-Hop Knowledge" gives a lecture of hip-hop's attempt to empower people. He cites everything from Afrika Bambaataa and the Universal Zulu Nation to the East Coast–West Coast rivalry and his own political evolution. The Universal Zulu Nation was an attempt to uplift the black community by encouraging clean living and empowerment. The organization encouraged a diverse membership and also encouraged economic, political, and social empowerment. The group incorporated Afro-centric ideas and also borrowed from the Nation of Islam. Although membership in the Universal Zulu Nation is small, it is devoted to educating people on the importance of "peace, unity, love, and having fun," in the words of Afrika Bambaataa. His history provides a succinct retelling of hip-hop as an educational form and illustrates exactly the ways in which hip-hop sponsors its own educational messages.

Part of hip-hop's educational story is teaching students of color the people, concepts, and events that they either do not get in public school or that are often discussed only in passing. Many textbooks leave out or frame in odd ways slavery, Indian removal, and massive resistance and often portray U.S. foreign policy as universally good. Woodrow Wilson's racism is ignored. Eugenics is only a vocabulary word. And George Wallace is someone who opposed civil rights instead of the more accurate description of supporting a state terror regime to violate black people. Hip-hop focuses on some of these issues in order to advance a version of history that recognizes black accomplishment and black people's important contributions to much of United States and even world history. This is an empowering corrective to the white-washed standard curriculum that portrays people of color as footnotes to their own history.

There are also traditional texts of the hardback or paperback book variety that tell compelling stories about hip-hop. There are biographies and autobiographies of rappers such as Common, DMX, and Prodigy. Poets such as Saul Williams often use hip-hop in their poetry. There are book-length projects available for political science classes, history courses, and English courses. One needn't convert a class into only song listening. Rather, a hip-hop curriculum could involve books, music, movies, and art. This is also important to truly incorporate hip-hop into the classroom. While hip-hop books and discussions are often about music, there are other ways hip-hop moves around and through popular culture, as this book illustrates. Educators will want to view graffiti, read free verse poetry, and think about what impact hip-hop dance has on group cohesion. Understanding the diversity of texts in hip-hop will help students understand that culture or aspects of culture are not reducible to only one form or understandable through the tools of one discipline.

Teachers often find hip-hop easy to pursue in communities. Field trips to a slam poetry event or to look at street art or graffiti are a lot easier and less expensive than the state museum or a trip out of the district or state to a famous museum or gallery. Communities not known for their urbanity or their diversity can still be involved. Small towns across this country have slam poetry nights at local coffee shops, and graffiti is ubiquitous in urban and rural landscapes and increasingly, often discreetly, in suburbia. For school districts or colleges short on cash and with students who have few time or economic resources, exploring hip-hop can be a lot easier outside the classroom than comparative work on European art or indigenous archaeology.

Educational studies are prone to fads, but one way to ease the seemingly whiplike movement from fad to fad is by slowly incorporating different texts into curricula to update learning without radically changing the delivery of material. Educational theorists and practitioners are easily swayed or at least so it seems when one reads educational blogs or listens in on a faculty or department meeting. One year it is experiential learning then immersive learning then decentered or student-centered learning then more technology then more group work then more individual attention and less group work. Much of this, as with changes in coaching staffs for athletes and high staff turnover in the workplace, can be disorienting for learners. Including hip-hop to liven up discussions and make concepts more relevant can help make transitions in learning styles less jarring. As much as proponents of various systems tout studies and anecdotes, they often fail to recognize that students struggle to change learning styles too. Including texts that make sense or are common to students can make that process easier.

Hip-hop also pushes the boundaries of what counts. By this I mean what counts as art, as dance, as music, as literature, and as evidence. Many teachers still have trouble accepting music as a source for an academic paper. Hip-hop studies argues that this cannot be the case, because hip-hop is a text like other literature, paintings, etc. While the veracity of a certain hip-hop lyric is always open for question, the veracity of sources has always been part of debate and academic inquiry. Graffiti challenges what art is. Is art only that which appears in a museum or a gallery? Do artists need training, the imprimatur of a certain school, or critique? Graffiti is often erased or altered. Does this make it less artistic? These questions are important for students and learners to consider, and a study of graffiti gets at them all. Hip-hop dance is taught in conservatories and gyms across the world, but does it count as dance for people's parents or for a ticket-buying public? The bump and grind, the Superman, and the Dougie bear little resemblance to the waltz or the tango, but difference does not mean incompatibility. So, hip-hop asks educators to expand what they think counts as specific types of knowledge and what is appropriate as an object of study or performance. This change is important, because students develop an appreciation for the ways in which their out-of-school world can help them in school. They can begin to apply theories not just to Greeks and Romans but also to the modern world. Hip-hop helps push education in rewarding directions.

Hip-hop transmits knowledge, and in educational studies hip-hop might be viewed as its own knowledge community. By knowledge community, I mean a community that constitutes its own rules about what knowledge is and how knowledge is shared as well as the hierarchies of knowledge and how knowledge is critiqued. Hip-hop often undercuts accepted signs of knowledge acquisition (occasionally preferring street smarts over book learning, for example). The emphasis on street smarts should be taught as an adjunct to book learning. Hip-hop simply encourages people to appreciate what they know and emphasizes that experiences matter. Sometimes this can be difficult to understand in the classroom, where one has to check boxes to cover the appropriate standards of learning, but after covering the necessary theories or dates, educators attuned to the influence of hip-hop will ask their students what those events and ideas mean to their lives. Although hip-hop is diverse, with many community members having under-graduate and even graduate degrees, one of the common arguments in hip-hop is the importance of lived experience. So, hip-hop artists may be knowledgeable about a subject because they experienced it, and that may make artists more knowledgeable than someone who has studied a subject or pursue it in a professional capacity.

Rather than rely only on history books, classrooms, the church, or the family as centers of knowledge dissemination, hip-hop itself disseminates knowledge. This is not to undermine the values of those other sources of knowledge, and indeed hip-hop often references them, but rather to high-light the ways in which hip-hop itself often proclaims to be giving listeners the truth. Hip-hop discusses current events (terrorism, political struggles, economics, party politics, social welfare policy, etc.) and critiques them. It addresses history, and not just its own. Students listening to hip-hop music are exposed to discussions of the civil rights movement, the Black Power movement, slavery, foreign policy, criminal justice, colonialism, economic theories, law, and more. Hip-hop, then, functions as a way to move beyond books as well as a way to gain knowledge that may run counter to what is printed in texts approved by states or school districts. While it is easy to think that a textbook or the nightly news covers all the important informa-tion a student could need, this simply is not the case. Hip-hop augments these traditional sources of knowledge. This makes hip-hop different from other musical forms because it directly challenges the politics of knowledge in ways that electronic dance music or country music do not seem to.

Models of work might also change in a hip-hop educational setting. Hip-hop often prizes collaboration. Artists get together to produce collabos not only in music but also in visual arts and apparel as well as book projects. The ability for disc jockeys, producers, artists, and artists and repertoire division representatives to work together is a prized asset, one that helps many suc-ceed. Schools that emphasize collaboration will find that their students familiar with hip-hop collaborations (Nate Dogg and Warren G, Mos Def and Talib Kweli, and more) may take to these lesson plans with vigor. The days of a romanticized lone guitarist are gone in modern music. Now people must work together. This presents opportunities for educators hoping to teach col-laboration skills and develop a strong sense of group dynamics and cohesion. If teachers can explain the benefits of group work in terms of how artists collaborate with clothing manufacturers or the way producers collaborate with their favorite artists, they may be able to overcome the often strenuous resistance to group work in the classroom.

Teachers across disciplines report success when using hip-hop. Companies such as Flocabulary have lesson plans and resources across science, math, and the social sciences. This company encourages incorporating hip-hop in a variety of ways, from types of materials analyzed to having hip-hop days of the week. Flocabulary argues that by applying rap to a host of different courses and subject matters, student engagement increases and students learn better. Hip-hop education is not all history and language games. In fact, this history and these language games can be applied to other subjects. So, students can learn figurative language because hip-hop uses it regularly. Students can then use those skills to better understand English literature, which they can then place in historical context and understand how language and historiography evolve by paying close attention to the changes in language in texts.

Hip-hop can also enhance study skills. Instead of the traditional set of acronyms and mnemonic devices, students can use hip-hop to rhyme their materials. Cadence or timing can be used to structure memorization so that students are better able to remember long strings of dates or events, much like many of us set to a song the names of all 50 states in order to remember them. The way one might write rap lyrics with a bar or measure structure might also help studying. The structure can be a valuable form of chunking by breaking down complex information into easily digestible smaller patterns. Without the skilled rhyming and cadence and an understanding of the ebbs and flows of music, students will struggle with memorization. Ask any K–12 student what they think of memorization, and the response inevitably comes back negative, but this is often because students have been given no strategies to memorize information.

The rhythms of hip-hop seem to reinforce memorization and certain types of learning. In the same way that mnemonic devices and the rhythmic rhyme schemes used to memorize information (the tune of "Old McDonald"), hip-hop's often beat-driven music may be a way to help students study. We all know that learners learn in different ways or, more specifically, that we do not have to force people to learn in certain ways. So, if studying to hip-hop helps one person and studying to Bach helps another, it should not matter. There are many ways to study for tests. Some people prefer note cards, others make online quizzes, some have outlines, and some use group study sessions. There may be methods that make more sense for the teacher as learner, but learning is complicated, and students do it differently. Students can do all of whatever works for them, and the results will follow. Study methods that turn people off from studying will never be successful. If we introduce hip-hop as a study aid, we might be surprised by how much better some students are remembering material.

Hip-hop can also give students insights into narrative. Not every hip-hop song is the drinking party anthem that hip-hop music is reductively displayed as. Hip-hop often tells stories of love, business success and failure, and neighborhoods thriving and dying as well as the stories of various personalities, personas, and people. Students may find that these characters look much more like someone they know than Falstaff or Atticus Finch. The narrative insights of hip-hop also emphasize fragmentation in modern society. That is, whereas the sonnet may not make temporal sense, a quick 16 bars may be easier to understand. The stories might also be more compelling. A story about failed love between two urban youths, a robbery gone wrong, a court appearance, or police misconduct may all be easier to understand than the complex familial politics of Italian youths hundreds of years ago. Sometimes it is just easier to understand the new version not because the old version is bad but because the new version is contemporary and more accessible.

Hopefully, hip-hop will be utilized continually in schools at all levels. It was easy for everyone's parents to dismiss new music from Elvis Presley to the Beatles to Motown, so it should come as no surprise that people will oppose hip-hop. Keep in mind that Elvis was seen as too sexual and that the Beatles' later work was criticized as being too drug-induced. Success often breeds criticism. But hip-hop opens up opportunities for students to experience the world in a different way. It can connect what they do at home with what they do in the classroom. It can introduce people to issues of difference so that they understand that not everyone experiences the world in the same way. The best educators will accept that musical tastes are ever changing and that many types of media shape how people learn and understand the world. While the Broadway smash hit *Hamilton* is often incorrectly described as a hip-hop musical, it did introduce to plays and musicals many people who otherwise would never have cared to attend a play or listen to musical theater. This is important. If Nas allows students to think about political agency in ways that the Federalist Papers do not, then why not include Nas while also thinking about what it means to vote, be a citizen, and engage in protest and other political activities described in traditional sources of political theory? Hip-hop does not have to replace the curriculum, only augment it. Just as slides, transparencies, and PowerPoint presentations reformed how people gave lectures and presented information, so too can hip-hop change how we understands texts and teach learners of all ages.

Further Reading

Emdin, Christopher. *Urban Science Education for the Hip-Hop Generation.* Rotterdam: Sense Publishers, 2010.

Forman, Murray. "Conscious Hip-Hop, Change, and the Obama Era." *American Studies Journal* 54 (2010), http://www.asjournal.org/54-2010/conscious-hip-hop/.

Hill, Marc Lamont. *Beats, Rhymes, and Classroom Life: Hip-Hop Pedagogy and the Politics of Identity.* New York: Teachers College Press, 2009.

Hill, Marc Lamont. *Schooling Hip-Hop: Expanding Hip-Hop Based Education across the Curriculum.* New York: Teachers College Press, 2013.

Mooney, Brian. *Breakbeat Pedagogy: Hip Hop and Spoken Word beyond the Classroom Walls.* Pieterlin: Peter Lang, 2016.

Ogbar, Jeffrey O. G. *Hip-Hop Revolution: The Culture and Politics of Rap.* Lawrence: University Press of Kansas, 2007.

Perry, Imani. *Prophets of the Hood: Politics and Poetics in Hip Hop.* Durham, NC: Duke University Press, 2004.

Seidel, Sam. *Hip Hop Genius: Remixing High School Education.* Lanham, MD: R&L Education, 2011.

Watkins, S. Craig. *Hip Hop Matters: Politics, Pop Culture, and the Struggle for the Soul of a Movement.* Boston, MA: Beacon, 2005.

Further Listening

Black Star. "Thieves in the Night," on *Black Star.* Rawkus Records, 1998.

dead prez. "They Schools," on *Let's Get Free.* Loud Records, 2000.

KRS-One. "Hip-Hop Knowledge," on *The Sneak Attack.* Koch Records, 2001.

Further Viewing

Morikawa, Keith. *Reading between the Rhymes.* Documentary, 2004.

CHAPTER THREE

Communication Studies and Hip-Hop

From the ethos of music to the ways hip-hop music and artists can be studied in the classroom to applying theories of identity, genre, and ideology, hip-hop has a strong hold in communication studies. As students and educators have been influenced by hip-hop music, the field is seeing an increased interest in using hip-hop to discuss issues of identity, black rhetoric, religious rhetoric, gender, and even classic Greek rhetoric.

Communication studies is a field as diverse as hip-hop. Communication studies scholars may have backgrounds in the social sciences or the humanities. Many study rhetoric, public relations, group communication, and interpersonal communication. Some scholars focus on specific policies, peoples, or types of communication. Many scholars study media including television, music, radio, and online communication, often called computer-mediated communication. Scholars of film and moving images have completed much work on music videos, hip-hop movies, and hip-hop artists on television. Many types of communication studies scholars are engaging with hip-hop.

Hip-hop and computer-mediated communication is a particularly interesting area of scholarship. On the Internet there are tons of mixtape download websites, message boards, hip-hop news websites, and artist and record label websites. It is so easy now to learn about hip-hop that while it has always been consumed at large rates by white suburban youths, now everyone from every corner of the world is consuming hip-hop. This means that hip-hop can be embraced without coming into contact with live concerts or mixtape sellers on the street corner. One might never know someone who disc-jockeys or raps. This is an interesting time, then, because one's exposure to hip-hop is greater than ever before even as one might be more physically distanced from actual hip-hop community members or performers.

Computers have made it possible for aspiring artists to take their recording studio with them. Now they do not have to wait to get elusive studio time and can produce their music in their bedroom or basement. This change to a more artist-driven model has helped expose more people to and involve them in hip-hop and has also meant that hip-hop is vastly more diffuse than it once was. Because hip-hop is so much easier to do beyond New York and Los Angeles, people are in fact doing it everywhere. Of course, the increasingly easy way that people can make music has allowed bad music (bad lyrics, bad beats, horrible production, etc.) to proliferate. So, much like people have to weed through shoddy clothing designers, poorly crafted movies on Netflix, and bad new restaurants, so too do people have to wade through hip-hop music of questionable value along any metrics. Nonetheless, there is something rewarding about making music even if no one thinks it is good, just as painting and journaling may be cathartic. Computers, then, represent a new and significant way to participate in hip-hop that continues to expand hip-hop's reach.

This move to computers is interesting for communication scholars because it allows for the proliferation of hip-hop and also connects community members in new ways. When the Internet was a new thing, it was common for aspiring hip-hop artists to post to freestyle message boards. Whereas freestyles used to be exchanged in person, they were now being posted asynchronously to message boards. Obviously this was an inferior form of the back-and-forth of a freestyle battle, but it helped include people who had no one to battle, those who had anxiety issues, and those perhaps unable to leave their homes or beds. In this way, computers opened up hip-hop to people with different abilities, which although often not recognized enhanced the community. Communication scholars are concerned with patterns of communication and the accessibility of interpersonal communication.

Computers make it easier to learn about hip-hop, communicate with artists and other fans, and produce music. It is sometimes easy to discount the impact of technology on music, given how easy it is to load music onto an iPhone or how simply streaming on Spotify takes the place of changing CDs at a party. DJs very often no longer use vinyl turntables, changing to CD turntables and then to digital tables that plug directly into one's computer and allow the scratching of MP3s. DJs used to need an extra car to move all their equipment; now all they need is a carry-on bag. These sorts of innovation may continue into the future, but it is difficult to predict what the next technological intervention will be. Advances are likely to be made in how multiple parties can work on music at the same time, changing the dynamics of communication that produce music. People will continue to emphasize digital exclusives and music streaming and downloading. The Recording

Industry Association of America (RIAA) now certifies music as gold and platinum both in digital download and streaming formats.

The addition of the RIAA awards for digital download and then streaming service represent two distinct eras in music delivery. The RIAA traces the history of its sales awards from vinyl to cassettes to CDs to the two most recent categories. In recognition of the changing way people consume music, the industry-leading RIAA may be a reasonable proxy for the way music has changed over the years. The change in awards recognizes how central computers are to both artists and fan life.

Scholars of rhetoric have completed much work on hip-hop. Rhetoricians often look at persuasion and social action, or the ways communication changes the status quo. Rhetoricians have considered the messages that hip-hop has promoted, the ways in which some artists make arguments about a range of issues, and the way hip-hop functions as a larger critique of society writ large. Because hip-hop artists are often attempting to persuade audiences on issues ranging from the importance of blackness, the evils of police brutality, and the dangers of gang violence to how bad some other rapper is, rhetoricians have found much to analyze with respect to hip-hop's persuasive strategies.

Scholars of family communication have yet to pick up hip-hop as a subject of study, but their work could fruitfully describe how hip-hop artists discuss families and also how these artists exist in families. Artists have long discussed relationships with women, their mothers and fathers, their cousins, and others. Hip-hop songs have taken up life with children, life with the extended family, and life in a nonnuclear home. Because hip-hop reflects the concerns of society at large, it should be no surprise that many artists address the problems and successes of their family life as well as problems that often exist in cities and with individuals from economically poor backgrounds. Many artists come from cities and poverty and are of color, so their music often reflects concerns of community members from these communities.

Hip-hop movies have also been studied from diverse perspectives. For example, the movie *Poetic Justice* (1993), which put a young Tupac Shakur in dialogue with a well-established Janet Jackson, caused quite a commotion as their love story played out on-screen. It also exposed a viewing pubic to a young, seemingly goofy Tupac, who seemed much different from the Thug Life tattoo-clad young man of his music videos. *Poetic Justice* showed many people that hip-hop artists were people, not simply criminals. As such, it challenged and continues to challenge the violence of movies such as *Juice* (1992), *Menace II Society* (1993), *Belly* (1998), and *Hustle & Flow* (2005). This violence, though, is not an appeal to our baser instincts but instead is an engagement with the world that needs doing. If we continue to act like violence does not happen or only happens to *them* or *over there,* then having meaningful conversations about violence becomes very difficult. Hip-hop movies help demonstrate the profound impact that violence has by fictional-izing events and relationship that bear a shocking resemblance to the truth. What this book has set out to do in a number of different ways is to discuss how hip-hop is bigger than the bling and the tabloids. It is easy to view hip-hop cinema as just another violent movie, but this denies the work's deeper meaning simply because it is violent. Yet we know that violent movies such as *Pulp Fiction* (1994) and *Django Unchained* (2012) have deep cultural rele-vance because of the violence they depict.

Becky Blanchard made the argument in an online paper in 1999:

> In conclusion, despite the blame placed on rap for the prominence of vio-lence in American society, hip-hop music is a symptom of cultural vio-lence, not the cause. In order to understand hip-hop, it is necessary to look at it as the product of a set of historical, political, and economic circum-stances and to study the role it has served as voice for those subjugated by systematic political and economic oppression. If the issue of violence in rap music is to be effectively addressed, the root of the problem—disparity in resources and opportunities for urban minorities—must be aggressively dealt with. Rap music is a form of resistance to the systems of subjugation that have created class discrepancies in the United States. In order to put an end to violence, we must focus on alleviating the burden of the inner-city working class. In order to put an end to the cycle of nihilism present in the contemporary culture of inner-city minority youth, we must provide them with the resources and opportunities to view the future with hope. (Blanchard 1999)

It is not hip-hop's fault that we live in a violent world. It is not hip-hop that has given black and brown youths a lack of hope. Capitalism is not a creation of hip-hop, and rap's representations of capital are driven by capital. Rap attempts to subvert these ideas, sometimes more easily and more successfully than others. Hip-hop's ills are symptoms of a deeply problematic culture.

For the viewing audience, hip-hop cinema was a confusing world. As white suburban residents started watching movies with hip-hop artists in them, they were confronted with a new world of inner-city violence, drug use, and black relationships. Movies such as *How High* (2001), a hilarious ode to weed culture, were remarkably successful. Not since the counterculture days of the 1960s and 1970s were movies designed for public consumption so cavalier about drug use. While certainly no cinematic masterpiece, *How High* did expose many to the world of drug use and the requisite hilarity that marihuana usage regularly causes.

Belly (1998) was significant because it was directed by Hype Williams, the most prolific hip-hop music video producer of the era. *Belly* stared DMX and Nas, both of whom were at the top of their game. Around this time people waited for DMX to release his second number-one album of the year. Hype Williams's direction proved that hip-hop directors could work in full-length film. Despite the success of this film, Williams has not directed another feature-length film but continues to work with musical artists. His most frequent collaborator is Kanye West, with Busta Rhymes a close second. Williams's videos often feature unique camera lenses and angles, and many are quite complex. "Diamonds from Sierra Leone," a Kanye West song, is quite arresting. It was Williams who made the fisheye lens popular. Here scholars are interested in the ways music, music videos, and even feature films may communicate messages differently as well as the similarity between the forms and the devices and styles they may use. That music videos remain popular, even as they are increasingly released online on websites such as World Star Hip-Hop, is a testament to the enduring impact of hip-hop on film.

Communication scholars are also interested in the ways hip-hop might help the study of identity. We know that language creates our world, defines our relationships, and builds and conveys meanings. Hip-hop, then, poses unique opportunities for the study of language and not just in the study of slang or rhyming. To be sure, this work is interesting, and the ways that different words may mean different things in different parts of the country is an interesting area of study. As a scholar, I am always interested in learning new slang from students and looking up a new rap lyric to figure out what the artist is getting at. Websites such as RapGenius (now Genius) feature annotated song lyrics, and users provide explanations (to varying degrees of intelligibility) for hip-hop lyrics. This sort of work puts people across the world to work thinking about language.

Hip-hop allows artists to tell not only their stories but also other people's stories. It allows rappers to assume personas or alter egos. They can rap about things they haven't experienced. All of these practices call identity into question. In a world where black identity is constantly under attack, hip-hop's potential to put black identity out front is a tremendous opportunity. Communicating one's identity is difficult. Makeup, lies, and false airs cover true selves. This is easy when one has the markings of power and when one's identity is rarely questioned. Yet for minority populations, identity is a particularly complicated and contested pursuit that hip-hop allows artists to play with in productive ways. Sometimes this play may be as important as any sort of notion of coming to an appropriate identity. The goal is not to achieve the most optimal identity for many people; instead, the goal is the opportunity to test the boundaries of one's comfort. This sort of work is important to steel oneself against constant threat and allows hip-hop artists to prepare themselves for a world that often seems to be positioned against them.

An interesting new style of music often derided for its unintelligibility is what is derogatorily called mumble rap. Mumble rap describes a form of rap with a basic rhyme pattern and the stringing together of monosyllabic words, rhyming ad-libs, and poorly enunciated language. Derided by some, artists such as Future and Migos have been wildly successful mumble rap artists. Scholars of language set out to explore this as a means of communicating as well as a transitional language form that has grown out of Atlanta's trap music. Why do artists mumble? Why use simple rhyme schemes when we know that complex rappers such as Earl Sweatshirt, Immortal Technique, and Chance The Rapper have huge followings? Mumble rap reconfigures what it means to rap and also defines a new style of rappers. Communication scholars worth their salt should be interested in new delivery styles and how those delivery styles reflect group membership, regional identity, or age. Mumble rap does allow us to break down the high/low culture divide that exists in hip-hop, just like it does in literature. We can question how we count rap as worthy or why certain ways of rapping are more worthy or better than other ways of rapping. Much of the aggressive anti–mumble rap campaign seems an awful lot like the language policing arguments that people made about hip-hop at its beginning.

The performance of break dancing, which has long been a part of the hip-hop music scene, also opens interesting avenues for study. Break dancing occurs everywhere, from the nearest local flattened appliance box to dance halls and hallways across the United States. Break dancing is a performance that both challenges regular dancing (a head spin has yet to make its way into ballroom dancing) and what constitutes appropriate action in a specific place. In the 1990s and 2000s, it was relatively easy to see in most major cities someone walking around with a skully (ski cap, toboggan, etc.), named because it fits around one's skull, and a large flattened box used as an impromptu dance floor, because break dancing on sidewalks and streets was dangerous if not impossible. Someone might throw down a piece of cardboard on a street corner in the middle of foot traffic, blissfully ignorant or openly defiant of street traffic and vendors, and people would gather around the cardboard. A dancer might engage in a routine or two or even be challenged by others. Break dancing often works like rap battles and competitive dancing that has been simplified. It is more organic than the cinematic depictions of dance performance in movies such as *Honey* (2003).

Break dancing represented a new way to communicate with one's environment that was fun, spontaneous, and fluid. Break dancing's vibrancy and fluidity was a reaction to the concrete jungle made famous by Bob Marley. Urban life in the 1980s and 1990s, and still today, was full of brutalist architecture, concrete, iron, and asphalt. Uncaring functionaries with rigid rules blocked public access to assistive services. Infrastructure was crumbling, as governments were more likely to fund highways that divided urban communities rather than invest in city bus services that encouraged access by community members to other neighborhoods. Opportunities seemed formulaic: go to the job or office and get the numbers of a bunch of companies that were not hiring, then stand in line here, there, and everywhere. City life could seem like an endless array of lines for no opportunities. Hip-hop and break dancing provided new avenues for creativity and expression.

Performance studies scholars, often working inside communication studies, focus on dance and movement as well as artistic expression. The menagerie of beats, gyrations, spoken-word pieces, paintings, graffiti, and other arts meld together to produce a number of different intersections of identity performance. Understanding hip-hop as an expressive form enables observers to see everything from clothing to dancing as identity making. In the same ways that high fashion might define someone in midtown Manhattan, so too do the actions that hip-hop community members engage in, say, something about their identity. Judith Butler, the oft-cited gender theorist who popularized the notion of identity as performance, emphasized how acts as simple as the way one holds one's hands to how one sits around a meeting table convey a performance of identity. These ideas help unpack hip-hop identity too.

A specific cultural identity important to hip-hop music is that of Latinx people from across the Latin diaspora. Many artists trace their ancestry to Puerto Rico, Cuba, and the African Caribbean. The RIAA has also begun to recognize the contribution of Latinx populations to music, presenting distinct awards for Latin music. Of note, the crossover hit "Despacito" by Luis Fonsi and Daddy Yankee was the first Latin song to be certified diamond. Both singer Fonsi and rapper Daddy Yankee are from Puerto Rico, and the award recognizes in some way Daddy Yankee's extensive work in hip-hop that has received little non-Latinx press attention. The increasing international reach of and involvement in hip-hop will continue to push communication studies to better research and think about diversity and difference in the industry and across hip-hop communities.

While "Despacito" was a bellwether for Latinx involvement in hip-hop specifically as well as music generally, the history of Latinx involvement in hip-hop is long. It is easy to reduce Latinx involvement to Cypress Hill, but this is only part of the story. Cypress Hill is certainly one of the founders of West Coast rap, bursting onto the scene in the early 1990s and popularizing the Los Angeles sound and aesthetic while also in many ways solidifying hip-hop's relationship with marihuana. "Insane in the Brain" (1993) propelled the group to national acclaim. The song, which according to lead vocalist B-Real is a diss track aimed at Chubb Rock, who had disparaged Cypress Hill's style, is featured in both video games and movies. The song's rhythmic percussion and B-Real's high-pitched voice became a classic at parties throughout much of the 1990s through the 2000s. The song contains many allusions and references to drug use, and the corresponding video contains visual effects that seem to suggest tripping on acid or mushrooms. The drug culture of the time period was part and parcel of early 1990s southern California party culture.

Latinx artists span hip-hop in years, styles, and messages. A short list of Latinx rappers includes Big Pun, Immortal Technique, Fat Joe, Pitbull, Joell Ortiz, and Chino XL. Interestingly, while many associated Latinx hip-hop with Los Angeles, many of the more prominent Latinx artists come from or reside in the New York metropolitan area. Increasingly, as artists such as Miami native Pitbull continue to dominate world airwaves, there will be an emphasis on Miami as a hotbed of Latinx hip-hop. Southern Florida, because of its proximity to Cuba and Latin America along with the large Latinx populations that live throughout the region, will continue to be important to hip-hop. As hip-hop continues to grow, more artists from underrepresented countries in Central and South America will likely make waves, challenging the dominance of Puerto Rican and Mexican artists. Additionally, Pan-Latinx groups are likely to grow following the success of Cypress Hill, so hip-hop may be a way to connect disparate peoples in the Latin diaspora.

Many of these artists engage in the sorts of postcolonial criticism befitting a Gayatri Spivak, Eduardo Mendieta, or Edward Said. Immortal Technique has been particularly critical of U.S. foreign policy and its effects on Latin America, a good example of which is "The Poverty of Philosophy," a reference to the 1847 book of the same name by Karl Marx. In this spoken-word piece, Immortal Technique critiques the U.S. colonization of Latin America and the country's extractive politics designed to take value from these countries and leave them with nothing but dependency on U.S. goods and services. The message is startling over a subtle beat that emphasizes Technique's words.

Hip-hop also bears heavily on leadership communication. That is, there are things to learn from the way hip-hop artists communicate and manage their lives. One lesson is that image management matters. Hip-hop artists work hard to maintain and promote a certain image (bombshell, bad boy, Lothario, gangsta, etc.). The success of those efforts helps them sell records and sell out concerts. Leaders of all sorts must also maintain an image. That image might be subject matter expert, cool person, genius, compassionate leader, or any number of other images. The ability of leaders to maintain a certain image influences their ability to gain follower support. Problems with image maintenance can cause leaders to falter. Hip-hop also teaches relationship management by encouraging people to be loyal to their family, friends, block, neighborhood, and city. This includes ideas such as providing for one's own, respecting one's elders, and taking care of one's family business. Leaders would be well served to follow these examples. Relationships matter in every industry and in every career path. Hip-hop also encourages being true to oneself. Leaders who are ethical, whose words and actions match, and demonstrate this to their followers always end up inspiring more people than do those who lie, cheat, and steal. Hip-hop's emphasis on being true to oneself is crucial to ideas of authenticity, trueness, and sincerity. Leaders who emphasize truth, honesty, and authenticity will likely succeed in their leadership endeavors, because followers consistently report desiring these traits in their leaders.

The diss track deserves more attention from scholars and hip-hop listeners. Diss tracks have been popular since hip-hop's earliest days. There seem to be fewer conflicts between artists now than from the late 1990s through the mid-2000s, but the back-and-forth of competing diss tracks is certainly an interesting phenomenon. We study arguments in academic journals and political debates, so why not devote some of these resources to studying how hip-hop artists argue? One of the most poignant diss tracks released in 2017 is Remy Ma's "Shelter," which disses Nicki Minaj with the deadly line "And to be the Queen of Rap, you gotta actually rap." The line started a Twitter firestorm and called into question Nicki Minaj's rapping ability and broader star appeal. The back-and-forth of hip-hop diss tracks is an interesting subgenre of rap that plays out like other arguments or at least deeply personal musically mediated conversations.

Hip-hop draws attention to communication as interactive, focusing on the ways that communicators respond to each other. Hip-hop considers language use and the way neologisms and wordplay can shape messages. Communication is a process that is both verbal and nonverbal, so hip-hop also asks students and professionals to think about what posture, clothing, and other markers mean in the communication process. Hip-hop is also theoretically rich, focusing on many of the ideas that communication scholars have about racism, colonialism, and even Marxism. Professionals will appreciate hip-hop's communication lessons, because they may be working with people with extensive experience in hip-hop and may also be attempting to appeal to people who have grown up while hip-hop was a top-selling musical genre. Ignoring these ideas when thinking about public relations, advertising, or even leadership communication is perilous.

Further Reading

Alim, H. Samy. "Critical Hip-Hop Language Pedagogies: Combat, Consciousness, and the Cultural Politics of Communication." *Journal of Language, Identity & Education* 6 (2007): 161–176.

Blanchard, Becky. "The Social Significance of Rap & Hip-Hop Culture." Ethics of Development in a Global Environment, 1999, https://web.stanford.edu/class/e297c/poverty_prejudice/mediarace/socialsignificance.htm.

Durham, Aisha S. *Home with Hip Hop Feminism: Performances in Communication and Culture.* Pieterlen: Peter Lang, 2014.

Maddex, Matthew. "Raptivism: The Act of Hip-Hop's Counterpublic Sphere Forming into a Social Movement to Seize Its Political Opportunities." PhD dissertation, Louisiana State University, 2014.

Sciullo, Nick J. "All I Really Need to Know I Learned from Hip-Hop: Hip-Hop's
        Role in Teaching Communication Skills." *Communication Currents* 9
        (2014), https://www.natcom.org/communication-currents?id=5217.

Further Listening

Black Star. "RE:Definition," on *Black Star.* Rawkus Records, 1998.
Common. "The 6th Sense," on *Like Water for Chocolate,* MCA Records, 2000.
The Roots. "Web," on *The Tipping Point.* Geffen, 2004.

Further Viewing

Dave Chappelle's Block Party. Michel Gondry. Bob Yari Productions, 2006. Video.
Rhyme & Reason. Peter Spirer. Miramax, 1997. Video.
Something from Nothing: The Art of Rap. Ice-T and Andy Baybutt. JollyGood Films,
        2012. Video.

CHAPTER FOUR

English and Hip-Hop

Long obsessed with the novel as the highest textual form, English scholars are currently looking at everything from graffiti (one of the four traditional elements of hip-hop culture) to song lyrics as contemporary narrative. This chapter explores the ways in which hip-hop explains the human condition in different but equally important ways, as with Ernest Hemingway, William Faulkner, or F. Scott Fitzgerald, and the reasons that English scholars are leading this charge. Those authors will always be important, of course, but when we only understand literature, composition, and the beauty of writing through archaic sentence structures, from dated topics, and from the pens and keyboards of certain racist, sexist, and homophobic authors, then we need to incorporate new voices into our understanding of the subject. Black authors of the city have long represented some of the most interesting writing of the last century or so. Richard Wright, Ralph Ellison, and Chester Himes are virtuosos worthy of more study than they currently receive. In many ways, today's hip-hop artists carry on the legacy of these authors. This is why hip-hop is so important to English: it changes how we think about writing, art, and language.

What counts as a text has changed radically over the last 20 or more years. Whereas many English doctoral students once aspired to study Alfred Tennyson or William Shakespeare, today such students consider everything from graffiti to hip-hop songs and everything in between. This change has led English studies to bridge the gap between the academy and popular culture, allowing English as a discipline to push back against criticisms that all it does is read Shakespeare. In addition, this change has helped English studies explain its continuing relevance to a world in which the humanities are under attack. Sure, studying English can help you write and read better, but not just materials that you might never need in today's world. It can help people decipher and understand graffiti in bathroom stalls and on train cars, as well as understand the music on the radio and streaming through our phones and computers. Unfortunately, many academic disciplines have to make these arguments now as almost any theoretical course is under fire as administrators push "practical" knowledge and application in English and virtually every other discipline. The turn toward studying hip-hop helps this by breaking down the high-culture/low-culture divide that has caused some to be suspicious about the utility of English in college.

Some bemoan this shift, preferring to stick to the canon, no matter how exclusive that canon is. We are fortunate as hip-hop scholars to be working at a time when the Ralph Ellisons, James Baldwins, and Richard Wrights are key parts of American literature. The acceptance of these authors has done a lot to pave the way for appreciating and critiquing black literary excellence. Were it not for the work of these authors, hip-hop would be set back decades in its study. While some advocates for hip-hop's study in English would argue that Tupac is Shakespeare, that kind of comparison is not necessary to justify hip-hop's study. Shakespeare and Tupac are different, and both are worthy of study in the same classroom.

It is not just English literature that is changing but also composition studies. Hip-hop has exposed students to rhyme schemes, wordplay, and even the creative process in new and exciting ways. Students learn about composing lyrics on documentaries and as they ride buses to and from school. A recent commercial for the Microsoft Surface laptop featured a teacher, "the teacher that raps," using his computer to compose rhymes by highlighting rhyming elements. The rapper's notebook, featured prominently in movies such as *8 Mile* and also central archival material in the Tupac Shakur Archive at the Atlanta University Center, demonstrate the creative process in ways that might be new to students. It is after all difficult to find drafts of novels to read aloud in the classroom. The call-and-response structure of hip-hop, stemming in part from the black church, also offers a new way to think about composition by asking writers to consider how the audience or the reader might respond and what role that response should have in composition. This is clearly demonstrated in slam poetry and comedy routines, both increasingly utilized in English classes as well as communication classes.

Hip-hop has always centered around writing as a creative process. Studying Tupac's lyric notebooks at the Robert Woodruff Library at the Atlanta University Center leaves readers amazed at the way one can read the revisions, hesitations, and emphases in his use of language by the pressure of the ink, a line crossing something out, or a change in phrasing. Likewise, a popular hip-hop image of Eminem on a bus writing lyrics in notebooks, made popular by the movie *8 Mile,* resonates with a large segment of the hip-hop community that would write lyrics on any surface available. Now this work seems to occur largely in the iPhone's notes app, but it still happens regularly, and I catch myself doing it as if I had a record deal and was going to be featured on the next remix of a popular song. Big Daddy Kane rapped about his lyric creation process that "Brain cells are lit. Ideas start to hit." He may be one of the first to use the term "lit" as a laudatory statement. For Big Daddy Kane, it was his writing and thinking that felt illuminated. Of course, this metaphor relies on the simplistic notion of the ways in which brain cells transmit electrical charges, but that is what makes it powerful. From brain cell transmissions to fires, the idea of it being lit expresses a kinetic form of energy that is both passionate creativity and a rocking good time. Big Daddy Kane is describing the tremendous power of writing for the hip-hop artist. It sparks the mind and is creative and generative.

The practice of truth telling resonates in English studies. One way to think about hip-hop is to think about its function of truth telling, an idea based in the classical notion of telling it like it is, a common rhetorical strategy. Truth telling is a way of directly confronting the world without the doublespeak of news outlets, classrooms, and other potentially sanitized knowledge environments. Truth telling involves honesty, vocality, and sincerity. In many ways, it resonates with Michel Foucault's notion of *parrhesia,* a classical Greek idea that means free speaking or speaking boldly. *Parrhesia* implies an obligation to speak truth to power, to be bold in the face of danger, and to speak in order to promote the common good. In this way, hip-hop's revolutionary ethos is a continuation of this popular rhetorical concept. Hip-hop promotes community wellness and uplift in the face of systemic oppression. It challenges the problematic ways in which welfare benefits are distributed and police pillage black communities. It takes issue with politicians and others who disparage hip-hop, the poor, and black communities. Hip-hop often recognizes that it is engaged in meaningful work that many community members cannot talk about on a regular basis. It provides an avenue for people to discuss issues of importance when they often do not have a forum in which to have these discussions. This duty to speak to the common good is consistent with hip-hop's ethic of care for community members.

Hip-hop has reshaped language. Hip-hop culture has added words now prominent across music disciplines and the world. Terms such as "trap," "ratchet," "gully," "twisted," "gold digger," "wanksta," "bling," "crib," and "lit" all have a hip-hop provenance or have been popularized through hip-hop. To be sure, not all hip-hop linguistic innovations make their way into the mainstream, but those that do often have a lasting influence. These new words, whether we like them or not, are part of a vernacular that connects hip-hop audiences across borders. These words often slowly make their way into popular culture. Popular culture often takes up cues from particularly vibrant subcultures, merging them into a broader cultural zeitgeist.

Lil Wayne's lyric "Real Gs move in silence like lasagna" is a prime example of how seriously hip-hop artists take language and wordplay. Upon hearing the line, it doesn't make much sense to most people. What do lasagna and silence have in common? Yet, when one has the line printed, the message becomes clear. The silent "g" in "lasagna" makes the point about a "G" moving in silence, "G" being the slang for a gangsta and silence being a sort of metaphor or analogy about operating under the radar. Real Gs don't need publicity, seemingly. This argument also emphasizes the concept of staying in one's lane or minding one's own business.

On the posthumously released "Dead Wrong," Eminem contributes a legendary verse to Biggie's aggressive, deep rhyme scheme. The complexity of this extra rhyme extends far beyond its William Blake–like imagery, which is impressive in its own right. Here Eminem is masterful. He connects animals with camels and mammals as well as the first sound in "*rabbits.*" That sound continues into the next line's "that," with the hard "t" sound resonant in "habit." One does not need to understand the complexities of language to hear the ways in which these sounds connect in complex ways to produce not simply the rhyme at the end of the line but also the internal rhymes that draw on consonance and assonance to make some of the most complex rap lyrics. The last line is equally as rewarding. There "lion" connects with "lying" as they are pronounced similarly, and "dying" obviously rhymes with "nine" in Eminem's vocal inflection. These sorts of connections and complex rhyming make rap so interesting because words that do not seem to rhyme are actually quite connected together.

Sometimes hip-hop artists change the definition of a word more than create a new word. For example, "crib" means a bed for a baby to most people but means home or house or living quarters to most in the hip-hop community. This redefinition can provide insights for students attempting to understand why authors use words in different ways, why connotative and denotative meanings matter, and even how to find their authorial presence and start defining words in their own ways. One of the ways students become great writers and great thinkers, particularly in the humanities, is by using language effectively and challenging accepted understandings of words and ideas. Hip-hop provides an everyday way to teach students about laying claim to language. They then begin to do what Jadakiss has described as "Y'all use beats for help, we help the beats." That is, Jadakiss is emphasizing how the best emcees control their lyrics as opposed to simply letting the beat or musical composition guide the song. He emphasizes the importance of linguistic mastery.

More than simply creating new words, hip-hop has changed what we think about composition, writing, speaking, authenticity, persuasion, argument, and evidence in ways that seem novel. Much of this has to do with the ease with which hip-hop is consumed and its portability. While New York birthed hip-hop, hip-hop is alive and well in Birmingham and Cairo, Paris and Long Beach, Houston and Seoul. Because hip-hop has taken the remix—the appropriation of others' words and sounds—to a new level, hip-hop presents fundamental questions about what it means to compose a work of music, to create a new artistic form. This means pragmatically that it is a lot easier to carry around an iPod than the collected works of Edgar Allan Poe. Even accounting for tablets and laptops, one can fit a lot of hip-hop music on a pocket-size cell phone, whereas books, even digital, seem to take up more room. Hip-hop's portability, then, is about not just file sharing but also the ease with which students can transport music from home to bus to school to sports practice and to home again. This ease of movement makes hip-hop attractive in the classroom because it becomes less taxing on student bodies (the image of the child or college student with a backpack half their size is a reality), is easier to share and listen to (phones and music players can be plugged into computers or speakers and projected in the classroom), and is quicker to read.

As mentioned earlier in this chapter and in the chapter on law, hip-hop has challenged what it means to create. At what point does a song become one's own? When is a remix so different from the track it remixes that it becomes almost undeniably different? Hip-hop's willingness to sample and appropriate words, lyrics, and beats has allowed hip-hop artists to do much more with music than was previously done. Far from the way white artists would steal black artists' songs in the early days of rock and roll, hip-hop artists often willingly acknowledge what they take as a demonstration of their musical knowledge. For example, DJs used to comb through record stores looking for the most obscure beat to sample, because their commitment to being "in the crates" was proof of their dedication to the art form. So, when a DJ put on a beat from a Motown song that might not have been a top 40 hit, the DJ and crowds would share a moment of acknowledgment about the discovery of the beat. DJs might announce that they were going to take the audience back with the introduction of a classic rhythm and then would mix in the acapella version of a newer hip-hop song before transitioning to a third track that blended the remix with a different song yet. In this way DJs might be understood as performing a literature review, paying tribute to the Marvin Gayes, the Sly and the Family Stones, and other artists who came before the newer sound. Such acts of mixing demonstrated a DJ's bona fides.

The DJ creates a new experience—one that connects old songs to new ones, expresses a continuity in music over the years, and is cognizant of hip-hop's origins. In the same way that one might start an argumentative essay by reviewing the literature, staking out an intervention, making that intervention, defending it from counterarguments, and summarizing and suggesting new avenues for research in the conclusion, a DJ might engage in stylistic practices that referenced a song's sampling pedigree, challenged one song with another, sped up the beats per minute of one song so that it came into better rhythm with another, and leave the crowd with a body-jarring head banger of an outro. The compositional elements are not dissimilar.

Along with questions of creation are questions of authenticity. Hip-hop artists often make claims about their realness or their fidelity to hip-hop culture. The final "battle scene" from Eminem's *8 Mile* has Rabbit, played by Eminem, challenging Papa Doc's authenticity by calling into question Doc's privileged upbringing, nuclear family, and elite education. These were arguments designed to destroy the eventual speaker's credibility. In hip-hop, interlopers are often understood negatively, so ethos is important. Rappers often work hard to prove their fidelity to the block, street, or neighborhood by writing lyrics that ring true. Authenticity can garner fans and can hedge against lyrical assaults from potential opponents.

Debates about what constitutes authenticity revolve around important issues of writing and speaking. How is credibility determined? How does one decide between two competing sources? In the same ways that English scholars might describe an author's voice as authentic if it accords with their experience or matches other well-argued voices in the genre, hip-hop scholars might describe a hip-hip artist's voice as authentic or inauthentic for the same reasons. A rapper who talks about the Number 7 train going to Brooklyn would be inauthentic because the Number 7 train in New York is a Queens-to-Manhattan line. Similarly, a rapper from Atlanta who brings to bear the production rhythms and cadences of other Atlanta artists might be described as authentic for matching generic expectations.

An area for growth is a continued attenuation to language use, because this will help people better understand hip-hop as well as other musical forms and language broadly. One of the most meaningful ways to understand a text or a culture is to understand how it uses language. Pursuing these scholarly avenues will tell us much about what hip-hop is doing to challenge language as well as reform it. This pursuit will also allow us a better understanding of what hip-hop is doing to critique and illuminate popular culture.

Just how important is this creative process—the process of writing? Rakim argues in "I Know You Got Soul" that "I start to think, and then I sink / Into the paper like I was ink." These lines focus on the materiality of the writing process. Rakim feels like he is "the ink." He is putting himself into his lyrics, sinking into the paper. The creative process is all-encompassing. He is trapped in the lines on the page. Only when he completes his verse is he free. These lines stress the creative process as a sort of meditation on trauma and struggle. It attaches the writer to the rhymes in ways that, in a world of songwriters who are not necessarily the rappers themselves, many hip-hop listeners may find confusing. Rakim was rapping when rappers wrote their own lyrics, and he masterfully centers the artist in the creative process.

These ideas stress the importance of hip-hop to English studies and the ways in which hip-hop might be used in the classroom and to discuss composition and literature.

Further Reading

Bradley, Adam. *Book of Rhymes: The Poetics of Hip Hop.* Revised and updated ed. New York: Civitas Books, 2017.

Edwards, Paul. *How to Rap: The Art and Science of the Hip-Hop MC.* Chicago: Chicago Review Press, 2009.

Edwards, Paul. *How to Rap 2: Advanced Flow and Delivery Techniques.* Chicago: Chicago Review Press, 2013.

Wald, Elijah. *Talking 'bout Your Mama: The Dozens, Snaps, and the Deep Roots of Rap.* New York: Oxford University Press, 2012.

Further Listening

Blackalicious. "Alphabet Aerobics," on *A2G*. Quannum Projects, 1999.

Jay-Z. "$100 Bill," on *The Great Gatsby: Music from Baz Luhrmann's Film*. Interscope, 2013.

Lupe Fiasco. "Dumb It Down," on *Lupe Fiasco's The Cool*. Atlantic, 2007.

CHAPTER FIVE

Sociology and Hip-Hop

Sociology's broad focus on and interconnectedness with education, criminology, anthropology, and other related disciplines has encouraged scholars in this field to look to various cultural forms for explanations of the lived world. Hip-hop teaches students of sociology about social movements, history, crime, law, and society and the evolving ways people express themselves, from their clothing choices to their consumerism.

If Max Weber is correct that sociology is "a science which attempts the interpretive understanding of social action in order thereby to arrive at a causal explanation of its course and effects" (Weber 1994, https://www .marxists.org/reference/subject/philosophy/works/ge/weber.htm), then hip-hop is a fundamentally sociological project. Hip-hop artists theorize family, government, law, relationships, social organization, geopolitics, and more. More generally, hip-hop artists are concerned with the ideologies, systems, and structures that order and disorder society. This focus makes hip-hop an attractive realm of activity for sociological inquiry.

Sociology might be considered the study of society or the study of social interaction. As such, its interest in quantitative methodologies often produces interesting results. Sociologists often rely on numerical data, study surveys, census data, and other numbers in order to derive information and build theories based on the sorts of hard data that many people regret the humanities do not rely on. By positioning hip-hop as a social activity, sociology recognizes the collaboration, crossover, and remix as tied to a unique form of sociality.

Hip-hop is also a fundamentally social activity. Artists and community members have affiliations for certain groups or styles of rapping. Emcees work with publicists, producers, tour managers, and others to become successful. Listeners attend conferences and concerts and share earbuds to hear their favorite artists. House parties often feature games, eating and drinking, and dancing as revelers listen to and critique hip-hop music. Hip-hop helps create community.

One of the most interesting developments in hip-hop's sociological inquiry is its theorization of place. By this I intend to signal the centrality of the area code, the hood, the street, the block, and the corner. In hip-hop many artists assign a particular gravity to place, and indeed much of the hip-hop world is organized around different spatial settings. Ludacris's crass "Area Codes" was played on the radio in a seemingly endless loop and encouraged listeners to find their area code mentioned, inspiring pride for residents who heard their own area code. Common's "The Corner" references Stony Island Avenue and South Cottage Grove Avenue, both infamous streets and neighborhoods in Chicago's South Side. He goes on to rap that he and fellow rappers "write songs about wrong 'cause it's hard to see right." Here Common interprets the corner as a place that is generative of the artistic tension between struggle and greed, between consumerism and the artistic form (hip-hop) that may provide for its undoing. It is also a place of wrong, a place where one must experience wrong yet hold out hope for right. This also answers those who argue that hip-hop inspires violence; artists are merely reflecting their lived experiences, which are sometimes "wrong." In the last verse of "The Corner" by spoken-word artists the Last Poets, they argue that "The corner was our Rock of Gibraltar, our Taj Mahal, our monument, our testimonial to freedom, to peace, and to love down on the corner." So central is the corner in understanding one's identity that it is in fact monumental. However, it is not unmoving. It is a testimonial and functions as a script or story of human agency and development. The comparison to famous world landmarks makes the local global.

Busta Rhymes's "Get Off My Block," which features Lord Have Mercy, centers the block but also engages in a complex analysis of spatial politics. Rhymes raps about a rocky interpersonal relationship with the pointed lyrics "when we used to chill up on park benches / My twenty-block radius." Here Busta relates the local ("park benches") to the global ("twenty-block radius") and stresses the need to delimit realms of acceptable interactions. The emphasis is on the permeability and nonpermeability of certain spaces. It might be easy to dismiss these songs as simply rappers rapping about home, but this undersells the importance of place to rappers and also seems to unfairly diminish the spatial politics of hip-hop while granting superiority to non–hip-hop expressions of home.

This focus on place should not be surprising. Much of how we think of the world is related to place. Voting districts and school zones are place-based. Public transportation and social services are often administered by place. People define themselves as being from a city or region, as living "inside the Beltway" or "downstate." These geographical markers of community help bring people together and also designate who does not belong. An excellent case study is the sprawling metro, suburban, and exurbian land-scape of Washington, D.C. Residents in this region may claim a specific neighborhood (Foggy Bottom or The Hill) and also may bristle when some-one from the city of Alexandria, Virginia, claims to be from D.C. The region is also known as DMV (for D.C.-Maryland-Virginia), but that name connotes all residents of the nation's capitol and the two states when it often denotes only metropolitan Washington, D.C. People in Arlington County, Virginia, squabble with people from Alexandria as well as Fairfax County, Virginia, in debates about who has the best schools, food, and libraries and who is more affluent, diverse, or in touch with Washington, D.C. The Maryland suburbs have a healthy rivalry with the Virginia suburbs. Exurbs such as Fredericks-burg, Virginia, often fight to be included in that amorphous region known as Northern Virginia, whereas people living in Prince William County debate whether or not they are a suburb or an exurb. All of this is to indicate that place matters and is complex, so it is no wonder that hip-hop addresses this important cultural idea and allows for people to express various geopolitical affinities.

This geographical politics draws on a history of forcible removal and dis-placement. Whether the reference point is the African slave trade (which witnessed white slavers destroying families and transporting Africans forci-bly across seas), the violent use of eminent domain laws, or Rudy Giuliani's "round-up the homeless" politics to clean up New York City, the history of minorities has been one of displacement. Thus, if the corner, block, or neigh-borhood can provide a positive sense of identity, a sense of affirmation and articulation, then one cannot help but embrace these spaces. Although these practices seem prominent in hip-hop, they are prominent elsewhere too as people affix stickers and magnets to their car with city and town abbrevia-tions and area codes as well as state and city flags. Place matters, and the politics of place in hip-hop are an affirmation of identity and self-worth.

Hip-hop also regularly engages the criminal justice system. Criminolo-gists have much to learn from hip-hop because it often conveys individuals' experiences with and in the criminal justice system and also because it might argue for different models of punishment, policing, and justice. Scholars such as Bryan J. McCann and Paul Butler have pursued such projects. McCann's most recent book focuses on the ways in which gansta rap was conjoined with tough-on-crime politics of the 1980s and 1990s. Gangsta rap was not simply proof that black people, hip-hop artists, and urban denizens were prone to crime but instead helped contest what constituted criminality and what the impacts were of claiming status as a criminal. Paul Butler's work has continually addressed the ways in which hip-hop functions as a critique of the criminal justice system and how hip-hop might lead to new ways of thinking about criminal justice. His work has provoked many responses and inspired a wealth of legal scholars to include hip-hop in their works on everything from criminal law to legal writing. These authors and others like them have laid the groundwork for continued investigation into the criminal justice system, with a focus on reforming a system that disproportionately incarcerates young black men.

Hip-hop has much to say about domestic relations. Several factors account for this. One is the complexity of the black family. For years reverence for elders was taught; that is, one respected and accorded deference to one's parents and grandparents. This has its roots in many African cultures where ancestors were central to one's lived experience. The destruction of the black family that removed the black father from many families directly impacted the role of men in the black family. Drug crimes, disproportionate and overtly discriminatory sentencing practices, and the oppressive welfare administration policies have exacted a violent toll. The criminal justice system has destroyed the black family.

One interesting phenomenon in hip-hop is the idea of "ride or die." The ride-or-die idea expresses notions of loyalty—either you ride with me or you are dead to me—as well as the willingness to put oneself on the line for another. This idea was popularized in a Ruff Ryders and the Lox song by the same name from the *We Are the Streets* album. In the song Eve raps about the virtues of staying with your man for whatever reason. The Timbaland beat and hook made the song a radio hit. There are a lot of reasons to be concerned about this song beyond the use of the word "bitch." It seems to suggest a sort of Tammy Wynette "Stand by Your Man" ethos that legitimates the acceptance of physical, emotional, and psychological violence. But the idea of riding or dying in this sense is more or less striving through whatever may occur to come out stronger and better. The idea is not that a partner should accept everything but rather that a partnership is complicated and that the best relationships exist when partners strive to overcome difficulties. As such, a "ride or die bitch" is understood as a supportive partner who embraces the challenges of the relationship rather than the passive Tammy Wynette antifeminist position. In the 1990s when many women were making substantial advances in hip-hop as lyrically gifted, sexually liberated actors in a complicated world, Lil' Kim, Foxy Brown, and others helped usher in a world of women who were in charge of their own sexuality, further expanding the idea of the "ride or die bitch" as someone who was in control of her own destiny—that is, a BITCH: a Babe In Total Control of Herself.

The question of the black family has been complicated in mass media reporting and from critics of hip-hop and black culture, and many fault hip-hop for in some ways contributing to what many understand as bad family values in the black family. That understanding seems to ignore systematic racism and the very real threats of poverty and violence that are directly traceable to white political action.

Some fault hip-hop for enforcing heterosexism and machismo. These criticisms are well founded. Hip-hop has embraced machismo and violence in part as a response to the ways in which white people have villainized masculinity of color. It was fine for white men to engage in any number of masculine practices, but if a man of color did it, then white people got nervous. So, there was a villainization of black sexual activity that branded black men as sexual predators and black women as whores. The woman of color as whore was easily transplanted onto Latina women and is egregiously represented in the tropes of the Jezebel and the Asian school girl. These mythic sexual associations have encouraged lynching and other acts of violence. The problem is that if black men act too macho they are a danger, but if they don't act macho enough then they're bad men. All of this, of course, assumes that there is a certain way to be a man that is exclusive of other forms of gender presentation.

Hip-hop often plays to these stereotypes. When 50 Cent would often don a bulletproof vest onstage, there was an uproar about how this seemed to condone violence. Then again, 50 Cent did not create the criminal black man as media trope. Furthermore, this sort of overidentification has a rhetorical purpose of making fun of media images. Many hip-hop listeners and community members understand that hip-hop artists do not want people shooting each other or committing crimes but instead are humorously enacting the worst images placed on them by an audience they are not particularly keen on reaching. The same is true for many artists who live fulfilling lives with monogamous partners. The outlandish hypersexualization of black men means that having a video with bikini-clad women in it plays to a certain audience but does not in fact represent who the artists is on a day-to-day basis. Understanding these rhetorical maneuvers—and of course not every artist is engaged in these more critical projects, as some do womanize, consume drugs to excess, and mistreat everyone around them—is key to understanding why hip-hop is not definable simply by its excesses.

The work of Mikhail Bakhtin helps explain this. Bakhtin was interested in the idea of the carnivalesque—that is, the process of using humor and chaos as a way to resist dominance. The carnival was an important place throughout much of history to let things go, be oneself, and live free of the dominations of the world. The carnival, then, came to represent a way to subvert dominant discourse by prioritizing humor and disorder. Hip-hop artists do this when they engage in the hyperviolent presentations on music labels, when they act the fool in the club, or when they say things to get a rise out of people in media. One of the best ways to challenge something is to openly subvert it. While there are repercussions to this sort of behavior, many hip-hop artists are able to weather those storms because of the money they have accrued from their success.

If hip-hop is going to challenge the arguments that people make about its gender politics, it needs to explain some of its stances. This also means that

DJs should give more air time to artists who challenge tired models of black machismo as well as mainstream media's fixation on the broken black family. It also means that women rappers need more air time and that instead of focusing on female rappers' physiques, which many of them encourage, we need to think about the ways in which being sexually powerful is a way to challenge how sexuality is deployed to control populations and degrade them. Artists such as Nicki Minaj and Cardi B are beginning to transgress norms of what women should do or should be in hip-hop for a new genera-tion of hip-hop listeners. It is easy to reminisce about MC Lyte and Yo-Yo, but many of today's hip-hop listeners have no idea who they are. That is okay. Clearly a sense of history is important in all pursuits, but we have to accept people as they are and help them think through gender politics given the reference points they have. The 1990s female rap era of Lil' Kim, Foxy Brown, and Eve was seen as a breakthrough for female rappers while also being criti-cized for promoting tropes of promiscuous sexual activity. It should be no surprise that these same criticisms continue to shape the way we discuss female rappers. Hopefully we will soon stop criticizing people for how often they have sex and for taking control of their bodies, and then we will live in a world where female rappers are judged by the content of their rhymes more than their clothes.

Hip-hop even influences foodways, what foods and brands are consumed as well as where they are consumed. Product placement is common and is an opportunity for artists to make money from their music videos. A manufac-turer of anything from cars to liquor to clothing might reach out to an artist for a plug in a new song, or an artist might reach out to a company in hopes of gaining some benefit from rhyming with that good or service in mind. In the same ways that television shows often reference certain brands in order to benefit from that brand with higher advertising fees or perks for their actors, so too does hip-hop have a complex commercial relationship with the products and services mentioned in hip-hop music. It is also not what is con-sumed but where. Hip-hop artists have played up cities, restaurants, bars, and strip clubs as venues for recreation. When Jermaine Dupri rapped about Waffle House in "Welcome to Atlanta," he was not only demonstrating his Atlanta roots (the first Waffle House is actually located in neighboring Deca-tur) but also encouraging others to be like hip-hop artists who after a late show or a night out at the club might get some good "drunk food" at Waffle House. Miami has always been a glamorous place, but Will Smith's "Wel-come to Miami" put Miami on the map as a hip-hop place to be.

In 2001 Busta Rhymes quite directly endorsed Courvoisier, a popular cognac, in his song "Pass the Courvoisier," which was featured in clubs through the mid-2000s. Interestingly, Rhymes also mentions Hennessy cognac, perhaps the most popular cognac among hip-hop artists, as well as Cristal, a popular brand of champagne. No strangers to commercialism and consumerism, hip-hop artists often promote brands in the hope of scoring endorsement deals and free products. "Pass the Courvoisier" really introduced the world to a type of liquor that was not on a lot of people's radars, a testament to the impacts of hip-hop.

This does not make hip-hop different from other art forms. Movies, television shows, and video games regularly contain product placements or cobranded projects (think Mountain Dew and the video game series *Call of Duty*). Hip-hop artists also appear in commercials as a result of their proven ability to generate sales. For Super Bowl LII, Busta Rhymes appeared in an expensive Doritos commercial, and Missy Elliott appeared in a Mountain Dew commercial. Busta Rhymes had already generated sales in another sector, so it is not surprising that he would be called upon to promote potato chips. Missy Elliott appeared in a 2016 Super Bowl advertisement for Amazon Echo, and her music has also been featured in Samsung ads. These sorts of projects illustrate a complex relationship between hip-hop advertising, economics, and sociology that many young professionals may encounter as they navigate the world of not just sociology but also marketing, public relations, and social psychology.

Likewise, hip-hop artists can be tastemakers. Ludacris's third studio album, *Chicken-n-Beer* (2003), prominently featured fried chicken, a southern specialty, on the album cover. Although the cover was subject to criticism, as it showed Ludacris apparently snacking on a woman's leg, the album nonetheless remained popular. He opened a Singapore-style restaurant, Straits, in Atlanta, closing it down to focus on and eventually open Chicken-n-Beer in Atlanta's Hartsfield Jackson International Airport. The seamless transition from album to restaurant is indicative of hip-hop's flow-centric orientation, the ebb and flow of not simply lyrics but also business and culture. Ludacris's restaurant is an example of the networked nature of hip-hop, connecting foodways to business ventures to albums.

Many hip-hop artists have turned restaurateur. Also, a popular Atlanta restaurant for 14 years, P. Diddy's Justin's, was a fixture in the Atlanta eating scene for years before it closed in 2012. The original Justin's in New York also had an impressive 10-year run. Not coincidentally, Atlanta's continued rise as a hip-hop mecca has been met with a rise in hip-hop artists' restaurants. T. I.'s restaurant Scales 925 was short-lived but received fanfare; Jermaine Dupri's JD's was similarly short-lived. 2 Chainz's Escobar Lounge is receiving early attention. Whether these restaurants have an influence on foodways remains an open question, but it is clear that the hip-hop restaurateur is a model that is here to stay.

Many of these pursuits suggest hip-hop's importance in business, discussed later in this book, but they also demonstrate the ways in which hip-hop influences society. Hip-hop is involved in how people organize, what they eat and drink, what they wear, and what they care about. Knowledge of phrases or lyrics helps demonstrate that people are in the know or are a member of the community. Certain clothing brands and styles express affiliation with artists, styles of hip-hop, or regional affiliation. In the same ways that live recordings of bands in the 1980s and 1990s demonstrated allegiance to Phish and other bands, having mixtapes on one's mobile phone or knowing an artist's current disagreement with other artists is a testament to one's membership in the community.

Hip-hop also spawns subgenres of independent artists and fringe performance styles. In this way in-groups and out-groups form. Rather than simply East Coast, West Coast, Houston, or Memphis rap, subgenres such as trip hop and fusion genres such as horrorcore also have distinct followings. Knowing artists associated with these various movements, attending concerts, and otherwise participating in these hip-hop subdivisions can solidify a group identity that is still hip-hop but distinct from mainstream hip-hop. In this way, hip-hop functions like other cultural forms whereby participation in countercultures or certain portions or segments of communities can have their own benefits and responsibilities.

Horrorcore experienced a brief heyday in the mid-1990s with groups such as Gravediggaz, led by Wu-Tang's RZA as the front man. Horrorcore often featured deeply disturbing and gritty lyrics about violence, substance abuse, and mental health yet was often applauded for more directly addressing these issues than other more mainstream hip-hop styles. The lyrics often evoked a sense of fear, becoming the lyrical equivalent of the slasher films made popular throughout the 1980s. These groups brought together the fandom surrounding low-budget horror films and hip-hop to highlight the deeply flawed present that rappers and hip-hop community members experienced.

Drug culture is another important aspect of society on which hip-hop has had a lasting influence. Of course, drug culture had its heyday in the 1960s and 1970s counterculture movements when Jimi Hendrix and the Grateful Dead made their rounds at concert halls and festivals and in everyone's tape decks. Yet hip-hop pushed drug culture to new heights, mythologizing the marihuana-filled production studio with artists and posses puffing on spliffs, blunts, beedis, and a list of names to describe virtually every style of wrapping, packing, and rolling marihuana in a smokable cigarette. As Lil Wayne raps, "I am a prisoner, locked up behind Xanax bars."

To be sure, marihuana is popular among many hip-hop artists and in hip-hop culture. References to marihuana appear in many songs. Marihuana leaves adorn album covers and artists' clothing. Artists are often arrested for possession of the drug. At a hip-hop concert one is likely to smell a strong odor of marihuana and see blunts being passed around. There are several reasons for this. First, marihuana is a relatively inexpensive drug and is extremely easy to come by. With an increasing number of states legalizing recreational and medical marihuana as well as a number of states decriminalizing it, it is easy for people with limited economic resources to acquire. Second, hip-hop's relationship to the Caribbean and to reggae music specifically explains the significance of marihuana. Marihuana cultivation and usage are common, particularly among Rastafarians and many involved in reggae music. It seems only natural, then, that as reggae from the days of Bob Marley and Peter Tosh to Inner Circle have influenced hip-hop, so too have certain cultural practices from that musical and religious community.

While modern-day hip-hop continues to reference marihuana, other drugs have also become popular and receive their fair share of references in songs. Jay-Z has an oft-quoted line in "Empire State of Mind": "MDMA got me feeling like a champion." This line is interesting, as it references MDMA, or Ecstasy (Molly), and the term "champion" an allusion to Buju Banton's smash 1990s reggae hit of the same name. In this line from a song testifying to New York's significance to the performers of the song, Jay-Z and Alicia Keys, and to hip-hop and the United States generally, the reference to MDMA and Buju Banton's classic hit connect hip-hop to counterculture and to reggae. This lyric then performs two important tasks by connecting hip-hop to a rich cultural history and a culture of opposition.

Famously, Lil Wayne's reference to "purple drank" has caused quite a stir. Purple drank is a mixture of prescription cough syrup (often with codeine), Sprite or other clear or yellow soda, and a Jolly Rancher. The concoction produces a strong depressant effect. Other hip-hop names used to reference this substance include "sizzurp" and "lean." The Memphis-based rap group Three 6 Mafia dedicated an entire song to the drink, "Sippin' on Some Syrup." "Sizzurp," the often southern pronunciation, also mimicking the pronunciation impairment caused by excess consumption, has caused several overdoses. Hip-hop's endorsement of different drugs does in fact threaten the unchecked consumption by fans, although we should not blame hip-hop artists for describing a world they live in or grew up in. That some artists may have engaged in unsafe behaviors does not mean that we should reject their insights or artistic ability to critically engage the narrative form.

Opioids are an increasingly large part of hip-hop; artists and fans use depressants at what might be considered a startling rate. Xanax (Xanys or Zanys), OxyContin (Oxys), and Vicodin (Vikes) are three of the most popular drugs accessible to large segments of the population. The most popular delivery method is snorting. Hip-hop celebrates the role of depressants as a way to escape reality. Using drugs is a way to challenge the law-and-order policies that decimated black communities throughout the 1980s. We can oppose some drug use and still recognize that drug use represents a psychic break with the status quo. In the same ways that a child acting out or a college student refusing to participate can send more radical signals about political agency, drug use can signify a deeper political commitment that is too often maligned as a mental or public health problem. There is a tendency to read prodrug arguments as endorsements of some romantic argument from the 1960s that imagines drug use as the key to political liberation. This argument, that drug use can be a political stance, is not necessarily the same as the argument that drug use leads to some better world but instead that in an oppressive political climate that seems to restrict the fundamental freedom to be oneself, one is left with relatively few options for doing what makes one feel good.

There is a danger that hip-hop romanticizes drug use, denying the impact that it has on individuals and families. Many artists seems to be aware of this, and it is important not to conflate artists' music with their life or their advocacy. Just as people on Twitter indicate that a retweet is not an endorsement, so too does the critical hip-hop scholar recognize that a rap lyric is not an endorsement of a particular consumption pattern. KRS-One raps "Instead of broadcasting how we smoke them trees on the radio we need more local emcees." Here a hip-hop original gangster rejects the commercialized obsession with drugs and promotes the inclusion of more local artists in the capitalist media space.

Tupac's lines "even as a crack field, mama / You always was a black queen," on "Dear Mama" sums up the complicated relationship with drugs and also complicates the idea that all hip-hop does is romanticize drug use. Tupac appreciates drug addiction as a complicated process that is not easily dealt with. He asks us to appreciate the person even though that person has a drug problem. The song spoke to a lot of people with loved ones who struggled with drug addiction. They were not bad people but instead were people with a problem. In this way, Tupac also makes an implicit claim that we should deal with drug use as a sociological concern or a mental or public health concern and not as a criminal matter. This places Tupac in line with many criminal law reformers who think that we need more treatment options for drug use and less prison time.

Redman also provides an early response to the fascination with drugs, a fascination for which he is also responsible with his impressive and extensive use of marihuana. He raps about his "high," saying that listeners "can't puff or sniff it. . . . I was born with it." Here Redman is arguing that there is something innate about being good at rap, or being fly. Quibble as we might about this sort of trait theory of hip-hop, the implicit argument is actually that one does not need drugs to be good at rapping, successful with the ladies, or famous. That is an argument that those who criticize hip-hop should be aware of. Hip-hop fans are aware of these sorts of arguments because they listen to not one or two lines but rather album after album of street knowledge.

Further, sociological theory helps explain hip-hop theories of social mobility. On the smash hit "Thrift Shop" by Macklemore and Ryan Lewis, when Macklemore raps about the come up as a found treasure that has meaning for the finder he is actually engaging in a larger metaphor of finding oneself and rising as a result. So one can be on the come up, or in a state of advancing socially, which is often a difficult existence to access. When one feels held down by drug abuse, poverty, race, or any other concept, the idea of having a come up seems quite idealized. When Earl Sweatshirt raps "Trying to make it from the bottom. . . . Feeling as hard as Vince Carter's knee cartilage," he is expressing a desire to move up and beyond one's situation. Vince Carter was once one of the greatest dunkers to have every played in the National Basketball Association. Yet as he got older he transitioned his game to perimeter and jump shooting, a reaction to the effect of age on dunking ability. Earl's sins weigh him down like Carter's knees do. Being a hip-hop artist is a mediation on what one can achieve, given racism and the visceral realities of urban poverty and an economic system that is never as meritocratic as it seems.

Perhaps one of the most interesting issues in hip-hop is its relationship to death. Biggie Smalls rapped, "You're nobody until somebody kills you." And while this statement is true in the sense that death often brings interest and occasionally acclaim, the way hip-hop artists have theorized death is incredibly diverse and interesting. Tupac rapped about Thugz Mansion as a new version of Heaven that was specifically for black folks. It was a place where "we could kick it" because there was "no heaven for a thug." It's the "only place where thugs get in for free." His alternative theorizing of Heaven is a radical theological rethinking of the world. If no place on this Earth or in the heavenly world was open to black people, then Thugz Mansion was a rethinking of the afterlife. Although we may quibble about the importance of an afterlife, if we can accept that theorizing an afterlife is good because it provides peace of mind and helps explain the unexplainable, then Tupac's Thugz Mansion was a rethinking of what happened after one stopped being black. It was a black future in the afterlife. That is meaningful because of how often every aspect of black life was taken away by white supremacy. It was not only that black people could not exist in this world but also that they could not exist in the next world either. Tupac's refiguring of the racist politics of the afterlife was a significant step in making a more palatable present. His philosophical thought is often ignored, but this is one way he was engaged in a complex rethinking of life and death.

These sorts of nonmusic forays demonstrate the ways in which hip-hop exists beyond music, influencing many different aspects of culture. A sociological understanding of hip-hop asks listeners, students, and scholars to think about the influence that hip-hop has across society.

Further Reading

Alim, H. Samy. *Roc the Mic Right: The Language of Hip Hop Culture*. New York: Routledge, 2006.

Sitomer, Alan, and Michael Cirelli. *Hip-Hop Language Arts: Thematic Textual Analysis.* n.p. Street Smart, 2015.

Sitomer, Alan, and Michael Cirelli. *Hip-Hop Poetry and the Classics.* n.p. Street Smart, 2015.

Weber, Max. "Definition of Sociology." In *Sociological Writings,* ed. Wolf Heydebrand. London: Continuum, 1994, https://www.marxists.org/reference/subject/philosophy/works/ge/weber.htm.

Further Listening

Jay-Z Featuring Alicia Keys. "Empire State of Mind," on *The Blueprint 3.* Roc Nation, 2009.

Kanye West. "Family Business," on *The College Dropout.* Roc-A-Fella Records, 2004.

Nas Featuring Lauryn Hill. "If I Ruled the World," on *It Was Written.* Columbia, 1996.

Public Enemy. "Fight the Power," on *Fear of a Black Planet.* Def Jam, 1990.

CHAPTER SIX

Business, Economics, and Hip-Hop

There are a number of ways that hip-hop influences and informs business. Obviously there are the artists and record labels themselves, which are subject to the written and unwritten laws of business. The streaming providers of music and music videos such as YouTube and Spotify as well as television stations like MTV and BET are all businesses subject to advertisers, shareholders, and other constraints and demands. Hip-hop, simply, is big business effecting in one way or another producers and consumers in a number of industries. Everyone is employing lawyers, security, trainers, and personal assistants. One's biggest economic expense might actually be one's entourage.

Hip-hop is a roughly $10 billion industry, a figure that varies constantly but one that nevertheless suggests a major player in the economy on par with electric cars and 3D printing. Many people are benefiting in this industry, and the more artists and consumers understand it, the more all will benefit. Business also has a lot to teach hip-hop. The more successful artists are at managing their money, investing it in their communities, and giving it to charities that sustain people across the world, the more meaningful hip-hop can be.

Jay-Z rapped "I'm not a businessman, I'm a business, man." This line highlights just how hip-hop has become a business. It is not that hip-hop artists are businesspeople but rather that they are businesses in and of themselves. This view radically departs from the desire to promote hip-hop artists as astute investors and business strategists, which is still important, and instead recognizes artists as businesses. This challenges the idea that record companies or talent agencies own hip-hop artists, repositioning the artist as a business.

All in all, record labels make decisions like other companies. They invest in artists they think will grow and produce many successful albums. Concert promoters hope to work with bigger and bigger names. Radio stations respond to listener demands and occasionally the pay-for-play scenario, whereby record companies may exert monetary influence over a radio station's playlist, although this is largely limited now and fiercely argued against by many. Just like one's favorite author might sign a multibook contract, so too might one's favorite artist sign a multialbum contract. When artists do not feel that they are getting their fair share in the deal, they might, however, put out bad work just to get out of the contract. Contract negotiations and the conflict between artists and record companies are legendary.

Relatedly, there is always much debate about who owns the masters. Masters are the original recordings of music. It was common that record companies would hold them and be able to use them for future releases such as greatest hits albums and other projects. But artists soon realized that record companies were taking creative license with masters and getting quite rich off artists' work. Record companies were able to re-release songs in any number of ways including new packages, and artists received none of the profit. This allowed record companies to make tons of money and left many artists quite economically impoverished.

It is easy to watch a music video or listen to the lyrics of a song and assume that many artists are living the high life with mansions, jets, multiple cars, and the obligatory diamonds and watches from Jacob the Jeweler. Yet much of this bling, a term used to refer to the shininess of one's accessories, was borrowed or leased. Many hip-hop artists never become rich in the classical sense but instead invest heavily in the appearance of wealth so that others might believe they are rich. There has always been this tension between what one's music discusses and who one actually is. That is not to indicate that all hip-hop artists are flaunting wealth they don't have but does suggest that it can be difficult to balance what sells and who one is, particularly when a record company is applying pressure on artists to do a certain thing to increase sales.

Bling culture has a strong relationship to questions of leadership. One way to measure success in hip-hop has historically been how much bling one has. Clearly, someone who has two Maseratis is more successful than someone who only has one Honda. Yet some artists have pushed back against this rampant consumerism. Artists such as KRS-One have been particularly sharp critics of bling culture. In "Classic (Better Than I Ever Been)," KRS-One, who became famous as a member of the early hip-hop group Boogie Down Productions, raps "I got no jewels on my neck. . . . I don't need them I got your respect." This indictment of hip-hop's materialism sounds a loud criticism from a hip-hop pioneer who has always maintained his authenticity and street credibility, eschewing the commercial path in favor of what many regard as a more genuine sound.

It might seem easy to reduce hip-hop to capitalist excess, but in light of the systematic exclusion of people of color from wealth, this interest seems entirely reasonable. When Nicki Minaj rapped "If I'm fake I ain't notice 'cause my money ain't," she put critics on notice that any claims against her authenticity were irrelevant because people were paying to hear what she had to say. Her position signifies the complex relationship between hip-hop feminism and capitalism. Minaj provides a way to reconcile the tension between hip-hop's consumerism and focus on monetary gain and other more theoretically positive associations. Her focus on monetary gain seems troubling from class-critical perspectives, yet her assertive and necessary call to be reckoned with as a rapper support the feminist hip-hop politics of many female rappers.

Salt-N-Pepa made a significant feminist argument early, rapping "You're just as good as any man, believe that, word." The message is simple and direct. As women continue to advocate for equal pay, many should be reminded of the direct style effortlessly delivered by early female emcees. Equality is a fight. It is a struggle to be heard in a cacophonous world of male privilege. Salt-N-Pepa are allies in the struggle for women's empowerment and equal pay because they emphasize the role of fighting for one's rights rather than sitting by and hoping for change to come.

Supply and demand still rule whereby artists in demand may flood the market with singles of mixtapes until the audience can no longer support the artists either with money or listening time. This means that artists who are popular one day may not be popular the next. Tastes are fickle, just as they are with clothing manufacturers, movie stars, and other products and services. It can be difficult to sustain a brand in a crowded marketplace. An artist must work hard to stay relevant and produce music that others want to purchase. Many artists are only able to produce one album that their label fully supports and publicizes before executives move on to the next artist or style of music. It can be difficult to get one's music out at a label with a particularly deep roster, so artists often leave labels and start their own so they can increase their control of distribution and increase the amount of music available for consumers. Although not a hip-hop example, I am often reminded of Sara Bareilles's smash hit "Love Song," which was not a love song in the classic sense but rather a song produced because her record company was forcing her to write a love song. When Bareilles sings that she won't "write you a love song / cause you asked for it," she is critiquing the way her record company forced her to write a love song instead of singing about a struggling relationship. Her struggling relationship was with her record company. Hip-hop artists are under the same pressure to produce more party tracks or more songs that will get radio airplay, so it can be tough for artists such as KRS-One and Common who take on issues of social import to get the airplay that their music deserves even while listeners may eagerly pursue their music.

Problems with earning and keeping money have generated countless news stories of artists who cannot pay their mortgage, tax bills, or child support payments. In some ways this is not surprising, because artists may not actually have that much wealth, most have relatively little education in business, and many people are trying to get a piece of the success pie. It can be tough to support an extravagant lifestyle while also paying all the people who help artists and providing for one's family members, many of whom seem to come out of the woodwork once an artist makes it. Just as it is easy to understand how professional athletes might have difficulty managing their wealth, so too are hip-hop artists often poorly positioned to maintain their lives.

Yet, hip-hop is rich in the ethic of hustle. Today's focus of many business schools on entrepreneurship can in part be explained by hip-hop's influence. No longer are students of the belief that a good education from a good school will secure them a job and happiness. Likewise, riding the coattails of one's parents is insufficient to make today's hip-hop–influenced businessperson happy. Business schools can and do use hip-hop to teach everything from entrepreneurship to branding, vertical integration, and talent development. In this way, hip-hop has changed business education to be less about winning friends and influencing people and more about engaging a new generation of hungry young talent.

Like it or not, today's young workers are influenced by different cultures than senior managers. Hip-hop may have taught some workers unhelpful behaviors and perceptions, but it also emphasizes hard work through ideas such as hustle and a willingness to accept change (flow). The movie *Hustle & Flow* demonstrates both these ideas.

Hustling takes many forms. It expresses an orientation toward the world, that of working hard. It also expresses the idea that one partakes in hustles, or side jobs. So, it may seem more common for biologists to also tend bar and sell handmade necklaces, for sales executives to also build and sell banjos, or for restaurant servers to also teach dance lessons and work as personal trainers. Whereas "hustle" was commonly used to describe what someone did in jail or prison in order to earn money or court favor, the term now refers to a broader range of economic activities.

Hip-hop is also a lucrative business for many people. Record executives, concert promoters, lawyers, brand representatives, and artists can often make staggering sums of money. Hip-hop is an industry that thrives and dives based on markets. When the economy is better, people can afford to download more songs and attend more concerts. The industry is replete with stories of artists and DJs working their way up to record executives, but the picture is not always rosy.

In "Moment of Clarity" Jay-Z pays homage to the "skills" of fellow rappers Talib Kweli and Common. Jay-Z expresses a tremendous amount of respect for the two socially conscious rappers, who are popular in their own right, but argues that he would rather sell many albums and make, by extension, many millions of dollars. This is a common debate: should artists rap to make money even if they do not care about what they are rapping, and does making money mean not rapping about what you care about? Artists balance this in different ways, as do many creative people who work in visual arts, advertising, and marketing. One might aspire to be the next Pablo Picasso, but it is easier to make money churning out print advertisements for soda. It is difficult to fault those who came from nothing, from a depressed socioeconomic state, for desiring better economic fortunes, particularly when they are from a minority racial or ethnic group and suffer the double disadvantage of being poor and of color. Jay-Z personifies this approach to economic advancement.

As with many industries, hip-hop does not reward everyone equally. Some artists toil under contracts that provide them with little financial compensation. Many artists rent the flashy jewelry and cars featured in music videos, being unable to afford even the smallest luxuries. For years, unscrupulous record agents conned artists into signing deals that made record companies rich and left artists broke. The "Free the Lox" campaign in the mid-2000s illustrated this point. In it, the hip-hop group the Lox (Jadakiss, Sheek Louch, and Styles P) were in an unfavorable contract with Puff Daddy's (now known as P. Diddy or Diddy) Bad Boy Entertainment and took to the streets to get out of the contract. The group distributed t-shirts and promoted their cause at concerts and other outings. The pressure eventually forced Bad Boy to cancel the contract, freeing the Lox to sign with Ruff Ryders. This is one example of many.

The "entourage" is another important part of the hip-hop business. As with most people who become famous in entertainment, hip-hop artists are barraged by hangers-on. These are the childhood friends, neighbors, and others who want to partake in an artist's success. Entourages also consist of security details, hype people (people whose job it is to get the crowd excited at a show), and runners who tend to the artist's needs. There are also the personal chefs, stylists, personal shoppers, nutritionists, accountants, lawyers, and other professional success gurus. It can be expensive to run a hip-hop artist's life. An entourage is not cheap, and one should not think that the people around an artist are there for free.

Given all of these costs, it is unsurprising that hip-hop artists often have trouble managing their money. Newspapers and tabloids often contain stories of broke rap artists. Many of these stories are about unpaid taxes, which is in many respects unsurprising. With many business ventures off the books and with tremendous amounts of cash changing hands, accounting can be difficult. Furthermore, many of the people serving artists are unsavory characters to begin with. Become a hip-hop artist, and rest assured that the one kid you knew in fifth grade who became a lawyer will call you wanting to be your lawyer. Because many hip-hop artists come from areas of the country served by poor educational systems and from families that may have been economically deprived, there often is not a base knowledge of how to manage money. Going from cutting hair one day without health insurance to cashing six-figure checks several times a year is a big shock, and one should not be too quick to judge hip-hop artists who have difficulty with money.

The hip-hop business is not just about record sales. Artists promote brands, perform at concerts, write books, and speak to groups. These other activities can provide more revenue than selling CDs and downloads. A popular artist's concert fee may range from $20,000 to $100,000 and more. Depending on the artist's record deal or even if the artist doesn't have one (artists without record deals can pocket much more of their concert fee for themselves), the concert circuit can be quite lucrative. More lucrative yet is the summer festival scene, where artists may be able to avoid contractual obligations to perform in solo or feature shows and net more of the money. This is why groups such as Outkast can continue to rake in money while producing relatively little in the way of new music. Loyal fans, like groupies of old, will follow artists from venue to fairground to college to festival with little thought.

Hip-hop artists have also ventured into a number of businesses, including restaurants, clothing lines, beverages, and other side projects. Sometimes these have been successful, and other times they have been quite financially disastrous. Hip-hop artists and community members seem to realize that even though capitalism risks derailing hip-hop's transgressive nature, that capitalism can provide immediate monetary benefits. The crude capitalism of 50 Cent's notion "get rich, or die tryin'" has been replaced by a more traditional and legitimate form of economic advancement. That is, hip-hop artists are buying property, diversifying their investments, and participating in legitimate businesses in order to expand their economic presence. The image of hip-hop artists as unemployed graphic artists or emcees selling drugs exists and certainly describes some community members, but hip-hop has evolved much beyond this. There is nothing about hip-hop that argues that people should not economically benefit, and as hip-hop matures, so do the economic pursuits of its artists.

Hip-hop is very much a mediation on capitalism. Without desiring to be too esoteric, hip-hop both exists in a larger global capitalist structure and often critiques that structure. This means that even as artists try to make money to support their lifestyles and families, many are also calling into question the very economic foundations that benefit them. Of course, students of the modern global business environment will recognize that these voices are already prominent not only in academia and the nonprofit sector but also in a number of businesses and industries. Recognizing this mediation helps unlock the potential for hip-hop to be much more than another way to make money. There is a tendency to view this sort of fighting within the system as somehow insincere, or at least this is often the response to many critics of capitalism. But I would offer that hip-hop artists who take seriously their role as cultural critics are adding to necessary discussions about the appropriate role of people of color in business and the dangers of capitalism.

Black Wall Street, made famous because of the antiblack violence that ravaged Greenwood, Oklahoma, a suburb of Tulsa, is one way that hip-hop connects itself to broader questions of business involvement and economic success of the black community. Prior to the 1921 Tulsa Race Riot, Greenwood was the center of black enterprise. White citizens slaughtered 39 people and injured over 1,000. The damage was so severe that over 10,000 black people were left homeless, and whites caused over $30 million (in today's dollars) in property damage. Compton hip-hop artist the Game formed Black Wall Street Records in homage to this tragedy. The Game represents the ways in which hip-hop often pays respect to black history, calling into being a historical sense of the continuity of oppression. The argument is not that the Game has told a better version of history or engaged in a radical rethinking of what it means to be black in a capitalist economy but rather that history helps inform the way black people approach the economy and also explains why many hip-hop artists are rightly critical of the U.S. economy.

Hip-hop does not suggest that poverty is a characteristic or necessity of being black or being a hip-hop artist. Oftentimes hip-hop artists who are successful are derided as not representing the streets or as selling out, but such a message misses the point and fails to recognize how important success can be in a capitalist economy in terms of advancing one's family or one's community. Successful hip-hop artists often respond to such criticism by stressing how their success is but another part of the long history of black excellence and economic success. The great kingdoms of Africa were thriving centers of culture and trade where many people prospered economically.

Now, Marvel's movie *Black Panther* (2018) represents a further telling of this story whereby Wakanda is vastly technologically superior to other countries. Wakanda represents an Afro-centric worldview by telling a story of African success when white influence was not present. As such, this narrative challenges what it means to be economically successful and critiques not those who have managed to amass wealth but rather those whites who would keep black people from wealth. *Black Panther* thus functions as a sort of capitalist critique that imagines a world where Africa's resources were not senselessly exploited by white colonizers and instead were carefully cultivated by black intellectuals, workers, and a black society that believed in building a loving, technologically advanced world that uplifted black people. This work helps reposition black people as potential benefactors of capitalism and also emphasizes that black control of the economy can produce significant achievements for black people.

One might cynically critique *Black Panther* as an appeal to a capitalistic system that produced slavery, racial discrimination, and violence without confronting these evils. The tension in the movie between Wakanda and the outside world might demonstrate this, but the sort of utopian theorizing of Wakanda as being immune from capitalism may be problematic. That is, an Afro-futurist philosophical orientation may be precisely what is needed to generate hope in a better future world, but it also may distract people from the everyday struggle of the present. Hip-hop is a necessary part of this struggle, of course, and hip-hop's relationship to *Back Panther* is underscored by Kendrick Lamar's curation of *Black Panther: The Album*. Bringing Lamar into the studio to produce this work stresses hip-hop's role in not only theorizing black excellence through Wakanda but also emphasizing that black people can make high-grossing blockbuster films with all the requisite tie-ins. The success of the movie demonstrates, perhaps as meaningfully as any hip-hop project, how integral economic success is to black excellence and how it is by no means anathema to the black community. In short, *Black Panther* imagines a world where black people are able to beat white capitalists at their own game, which is a biting critique of the economic system that seems to have substantially disfavored people of color since the creation of the United States.

Big L delivered a poignant critique of neoliberalism with his now classic line "I wasn't poor, I was po, I couldn't afford the o-r." Big L recasts the question of poverty as not simply a capitalist problem but one that itself is linguistically structured. There were poor people then there were po people, enacting a common black pronunciation of "poor" as a reference to both the long history of urban black poverty and the ways poverty is linguistically constructed. One could be poor, but one never wanted to be po. It is easy to dismiss such lines as one-off criticism, but they represent astute critiques of the world in which hip-hop artists live.

One of the ways hip-hop will need to grow is that people will need to make sure artists are using their money responsibly. Hip-hop artists, like much of the nouveau riche, will need to devote resources to money management and wealth protection. Just as athletes have realized over the last 30 years that money does not last forever and have subsequently gone to great lengths to protect their money, so too will hip-hop artists need to do some financial planning. One of the ways business will grow with hip-hop is that financial services will need to devote more time and expertise to hip-hop. Financial planners will need to read up on royalties, and hip-hop artists will need to think about diversifying their portfolios. Far from being pejorative, this suggestion is simply to note that financial education will radically improve the financial lot of hip-hop artists.

Managers and leaders, who are often not the same, will need to account for the influence of hip-hop on those who work for them and whom they lead. This may require a rethinking of what management and leadership is.

This does not necessarily mean rethinking how business is done, although many managers are doing just that. Let's consider the five new realities of leadership communication that Boris Groysberg and Michael Slind identify in the June 2012 issue of the *Harvard Business Review:* economic change (focus on the service industry), organizational change (less hierarchy), global change (diversity), generational change (millennials), and technological change (social media). Hip-hop impacts each of these areas. The focus on the service industry means that customer service will drive the economy. It also means that consumers will shape the music industry. These consumers will demand not only quality but also quantity of production. This is why so many artists intersperse their albums with mixtape releases. Likewise, managers may find that their employees gather more value from their side hustles (mixtapess) than their 9–5 work (albums). Many workers may enjoy working as the assistant baseball coach for the high school more than being a staff accountant. Managers who allow longer and later lunches so that an employee might be able to make it to practice three days per week will find that employee much more motivated to work at the regular job. The flattening of jobs such that 360 degree feedback is the norm and that teams are often made of diverse employees will mean that employees expect to be included in the production of reports and even in the making of company-wide decisions. Hip-hop flattens as well, with collaborations being heralded. The global nature of business resonates with the global nature of hip-hop. Employees may be as versed in Toronto hip-hop as they are in local transportation funding, and bosses who appreciate this may be willing to accept that a diversity of ideas exists in the workplace. Without being too reductive, the boss who orders poutine, which is featured as a cultural reference in Canadian hip-hop, for the next company lunch and says to the employee "I know you like Canadian hip-hop, but the best I could do is Canadian poutine" will likely score points as someone who cares about their workers. This also means that people get their ideas from a wider array of sources. Rather than ABC, NBC, and CBS nightly newscasts, workers may be more influenced by what a certain rapper says. Millennials are filling jobs in countless industries. As a whole, they buy and listen to a lot of hip-hop. This doesn't mean inviting Chance The Rapper to be the company picnic's keynote speaker, but it does mean letting employees listen to hip-hop at their desks even if the lyrics might contain a curse word. Likewise, hip-hop has embraced social media. Many younger employees are much more technologically savvy than their employers. Allowing these employees to take charge of these efforts can dramatically improve a social media presence that consisted mostly of company earnings reports and announcements of new advertisements prior to a more tech-savvy employee's inclusion. That is, hip-hop can help managers understand and adapt to the changing economy and the changing workforce. Both will improve the bottom line and will also improve employee retention.

Hip-hop does occasionally provide an important narrative to challenge the depressing stories featured on the nightly news. Hip-hop recasts the hood as a place of possibility, experiences, and street smarts as a necessary skill for a successful life. Horatio Alger success stories are not the universal standard that they once were. The best success narrative might be one's friend who was able to work as a rapper's hype man. It might be the person who went to a rival high school and released an extended play record. Hip-hop provides these stories, and they can be as inspiring as any classic novel or short story. For those people looking for inspiration, Bill Gates or other business moguls may not seem accessible. A rapper from the same neighborhood who went to the same public school or whose grandmother lived on the same street might be a much more attractive role model precisely because the rapper seems more like the average person. A common criticism of many forms of education is that they idolize the excellent. If all students do is try to make as much as Bill Gates, write as crisply as Ernest Hemingway, or speak with the moral force of Martin Luther King Jr., they can feel a sense of failure when they do not achieve those ends. But if teachers reframe learning so that it is about actual people from the city or about people who may not have made billions but did manage to sign a record deal that lets them afford a home and a car, they might ultimately encourage more students to take their studies seriously. In business this can be an empowering message of success that really embraces success and possibility.

Further Reading

Charnas, Dan. *The Big Payback: The History of the Business of Hip-Hop.* New York: Penguin, 2010.

Harris, T. Brookshire. *Billionaire Branding: How Hip Hop's Cash Kings Built Their Empires.* Raleigh, NC: Brookshire Book Group, 2016.

King, Curtiss. *The Prosperous Hip Hop Producer: My Beat-Making Journey from My Grandma's Patio to a Six-Figure Business.* Anna Marie, FL: Maurice Bassett, 2018.

Miller, Giles. *Everything I Need to Know about Business I Learned from Hip-Hop: A Millennial's Guide to Making Bank.* Naperville, IL: Hesketh Giles Miller.

Further Listening

DJ Khalid. "All I Do Is Win," on *Victory.* We the Best Music Group, 2010.

Drake and Trey Songz. "Successful," on *So Far Gone.* October's Very Own, 2009.

50 Cent. "I Get Money," on *Curtis.* Shady Records, 2007.

T. I. "Whatever You Like," on *Paper Trail.* Grand Hustle Records, 2008.

CHAPTER SEVEN

Religion and Hip-Hop

An often unexplored area of culture is religion. There are probably many reasons for this. Religious conversations can be quite uncomfortable, just like political conversations. Although many people, particularly in academia, are emphasizing the importance of interfaith dialogue, many people claim to be not religious or not actively attending church or religious services. This seems true particularly among high school and college students who, according to surveys, are less religious now than they have been. Yet we know that religion is important to many in the United States irrespective of their particular faith. The news media regularly reports on Islamic extremism as well as various faith celebrations. There are active debates about how people should celebrate Christmas and if there should be state-supported displays celebrating Christmas. While many Muslims have felt discriminated against following the terrorist attacks of September 11, 2001, many atheists feel discriminated against because of how critical people are of their lack of faith. Many colleges and universities, local governments, and other institutions subtly and not so subtly reinforce Christian beliefs to the exclusion of atheists, Muslims, and Jews. Religious debates rage on.

Reverend Stephen Pogue argued in a 2006 National Public Radio segment that "Hip-hop is a culture, and we needed to reach people in that culture with the Gospel of Jesus Christ. So that's what we're really trying to do to reach a people and a culture that the church had really just overlooked. It gives the young people an opportunity to take ownership of a worship experience." In this sense, hip-hop does not pervert religion or religious messages; instead, it is a way to reach people whom religious messages have failed to reach. For hard-liners and traditionalists this argument fails, but for those interested in expanding the reach of religious teachings, it makes sense as another option in forming a persuasive, inclusive ministry.

Unpacking the role of religion in culture takes time, because people have dug in on all possible sides. The unreflective position that religion does not matter is equally as destructive as the position that understands religion's influence on all aspects of life. Both sides should move back from these dangerous positions. Religion can affect and be affected by aspects of culture without it being the defining positive or negative aspect of any culture. Claims of religion's defining influence on culture seem to ignore the importance not of secularism but rather of atheism. Secularism is the division between religion and the state. Most people would argue that the United States is or at least claims to be a secular country. The veracity of that claim is of course debatable. Yet, many people know little of atheism and would bristle at the idea that many others are able to go through life without religion and without much religious influence.

Hip-hop brings an interest in religion that draws on the tradition of the black church and the Negro spiritual. Hip-hop also incorporates Islamic beliefs, various Christian beliefs, and even African-based religious beliefs. Hip-hop's religious orientations are as diverse as the world's. Much popular music seems to focus on Christian beliefs. There is even a sizable subgenre of music called Christian hip-hop. There are countless mentions of the Christian God, the Bible, and religious ideas about salvation, atonement, sacrifice, and praying. The development of Christian themes—and most of the themes are Christian—is common in hip-hop, and the success of hip-hop as a cultural form has encouraged churches to incorporate it into their services. While the sort of new age Christian church service is often represented by the singer-songwriter or rock genres in the popular imagination, increasingly rap is replacing rock as the preferred genre to reach younger church members. Obviously this changes depending on demographics and church doctrine, but rap has a role in Christianity. Savvy ministers are using it with great success.

The Christian publisher InterVarsity has published Efrem Smith and Phil Jackson's book *The Hip-Hop Church: Connecting with the Movement Shaping Our Culture,* which argues that churches need to accept and embrace hip-hop rather than shun it. The authors encourage the acceptance of hip-hop churches and argue that many hip-hop churches are succeeding because of their acceptance and utilization of break dancing, DJing, and rapping as opposed to traditional readings of the Gospels and other common religious messaging. Smith and Jackson also argue that hip-hop can communicate religious messages and has its own religious messaging. Both are important ways of thinking about hip-hop in the multimediated world. Likewise, Daniel White Hodge has argued in his book *The Soul of Hip Hop: Rims, Timbs and a Cultural Theology* that hip-hop has a recognizable theological center. Hodge's argument seems as though he is trying to force hip-hop into a theological space that many in the hip-hop community would find reductive and uncritical, but his argument is nonetheless an important way to think about hip-hop's theological roots. While his approach is aggressive and deterministic, Hodge nonetheless demonstrates that there is an exchange between hip-hop and religion worthy of further study and one certainly important for cultural theorists and critical thinkers.

Take Crossover Church in Tampa, Florida, as an example. The church touts a multiethnic, multigenerational crowd and includes spoken word, dance, R&B, reggae, and rap in its services. The church even spells its kids ministry with a "z"—Kidz Ministry. Tampa, a racially diverse southern city, has an active hip-hop community, including T-Pain. All of these are attempts to appeal to a young, urban, racially diverse audience. While it is easy to dismiss efforts such as this as shallow attempts to sway the public, many churches are pursuing similar paths because there is nothing antithetical about hip-hop and Christianity.

The Pew Research Center has found that people 18 to 29 years old are less religious than older folks. There are many reasons for this. Church plays less of a role in people's lives, including older generations who go to church less often. Religion is taught less in schools and in colleges. In addition, religion is often associated with a lack of education and critical thinking as a result of substantial criticism in the public sphere. Churches were slow to embrace modern trends in media usage, and as a result people became less interested in churches that did not seem to keep up with modern theories about culture and education. Many religious institutions also did a poor job explaining why religion matters in public life, given that people were working longer hours and their children were involved in more after-school activities. When other clubs and organizations offer everything from free food to networking to professional development, many of the things that churches would provide, many students went to other organizations for those things. This is not because church failed at doing those things but rather that other organizations made more compelling cases, so high school and college students joined fraternities, environmental clubs, and political organizations. Some might bristle at the idea that religion failed on these fronts, but these failures are certainly one of the reasons why church membership and religiosity declined. Interestingly, partly because of the busy lives that people are living, many people on social media seem to espouse nonchurch-centered theologies and spiritualities. In this way church membership may have declined, while spirituality may remain constant. No matter the causes, many churches are scrambling to attract this age range, and hip-hop seems to be one way to do that.

Aaron Earls argues in a 2016 blog post that there are five reasons for church leaders to pay attention to hip-hop. The first is cultural understanding. Earls argues that more people are listening to hip-hop than many other forms of music, something that for years data has supported. Understanding hip-hop can help church leaders understand millennials and other younger parishioners. Just as this book hopes to help people understand hip-hop so they can relate to the changing cultural landscape, so too can church leaders benefit from understanding what people are listening to. Second, understanding hip-hop can help people understand communication. Communicating to young churchgoers means not simply using slang or tweeting but instead understanding what people mean when they speak or write. It means understanding that people communicate differently and understand communication differently. Church leaders do not need to rap their sermons, but they do need to be aware that their church members may be less persuaded by the King James Bible than they were before. Language changes, and people's ability or interest in understanding texts or speaking in ways that were popular only a few years before changes. Third, hip-hop often brings different perspectives to people's lives. Hip-hop exposes people to race, class, and gender issues in ways that may be uncomfortable. Hip-hop may raise issues that were not previously considered by church leaders. In short, hip-hop can help church leaders understand the diversity of experiences in their congregations. Fourth, hip-hop can be about religion, and therefore studying hip-hop gives new insight into theological conversations. Kanye West famously called one of his albums a gospel album. So, even without scripture or homilies, rap can provide theological insights. Fifth, hip-hop can provide reminders about the importance of religion, something that members of the clergy often need to sustain their work. Earls's arguments should resonate with church leaders, as he is arguing for continuing the Christian mission by expanding the ways in which one appreciates Christianity.

One of the obvious connections between religion and hip-hop is that they both emphasize the oral tradition. The earliest religious traditions were oral, and much of the way people came to understand modern Islam or Christianity was from what others told them, not what was written down in any book. Today, while Bible studies are common, people still flock to churches and other religious institutions to hear priests, pastors, imams, rabbis, and others speak about religion. The oral tradition matters, and the best rappers and preachers are often those who have a flair for oral delivery. Part of Tupac's appeal is his gravelly voice in the same way that Martin Luther King Jr.'s appeal is not simply the gravity of his messages but also the way he spoke, honed from years of practice in churches in Atlanta and Alabama. This oral connection will continue to be important and will be one of the ways that church leaders make the argument for hip-hop coming into church.

One of the greatest rappers of Christian theology was Tupac Shakur. He had a preoccupation with death that seemed almost pathological. Many of his songs deal with the inevitability of death and the necessity of having to contemplate what comes after death. Tupac's Christianity was eschatological. In "Thugz Mansion" Tupac visualized a special afterlife distinct from white

Heaven called Thugz Mansion. He described it as "a spot where we can kick it. . . . A spot where we belong." Here Tupac argues for a special place where thugs, or black people, can be themselves. This is a place where they need not worry about racism or overpolicing and can be themselves without the judgment and violence of the world they experience on Earth. He identifies many of the struggles of street life and their deleterious effects, and he longingly imagines a better netherworld. This song pulls on similar themes from Tupac's early release "I Ain't Mad at Cha" (1996), which emphasizes the resilience of friendship through death and fame, and a video that features Tupac rapping from Heaven. In the video Tupac's bars from Heaven seem to foreshadow his own death, and the song was released two days after he died.

Tupac's preoccupation with death should not be surprising. Keep in mind that young black men die at an astounding rate and one much greater than their white counterparts. Poverty, of course, exacerbates mortality rates. So, a preoccupation with death and attempts to explain it, to cope with it, are rational responses. People often find religion in times of need, so coupled with the prevalence of the black church, hip-hop's interest in religion and spirituality are a continuation of the broader sustaining role of religion in black life.

DMX includes biblical allusions in many of his albums. His "Lord Give Me a Sign" (2006) is a song about attempting to live a good life in spite of the world's trials and tribulations. The song's aggressive beat underscores the difficulties of living a righteous life with the violence and temptations of urban life ever present. His albums often feature a song called "Prayer" in which he meditates on religion and his attempts to live a good life. This theme, trying to live a righteous life, is common. Hip-hop artists often struggle in the push and pull of street life no matter how monetarily successful they have become.

DMX presents an interesting case, however, and illustrates why many religious people are dubious about hip-hop's importance to religion. DMX has had more than his fair share of run-ins with law. In fact, he has faced everything from tax problems to drug problems. These issues are counterimposed on his religious messages. On the same albums where he is arguing for a better understanding of God, he is also talking about having sex with numerous women, using drugs, and committing violent crime. Although hip-hop scholars often make the "don't throw the baby out with the bathwater" argument, one has to be a critical listener as well. While it is often easy to give advice about how one can try to live a righteous life, how convincing or persuasive is someone who does not do that? Hip-hop artists struggle with these ideas. Of course, it is not as if overpolicing does not exacerbate these problems. While it is fairly easy to walk down the street with a joint anywhere in the country, urban populations are often the victim of stop-and-frisk policies that give police wide latitude to stop anyone in the street and frisk them. More reason to pray, no doubt.

Kanye West's "Jesus Walks" (2004) is a prime example of religious hip-hop, equally lauded for the seriousness it brought to religious discussions and critiqued for the controversial images of him perhaps positioning himself as Jesus in the music video. Some critics thought that Kanye was making light of the crucifixion story, whereas others were eager to have hip-hop artists make some comment on religion. Either way, the song was critically lauded for taking up religious, racial, and economic themes at a time in the early 2000s when many people were torn between some seeming economic prosperity and the increasing size of the police state.

Law professor SpearIt has taken up the importance of hip-hop and Islam particularly for incarcerated individuals. He argues that hip-hop frames discussions of mass incarceration as being analogous to slavery and replicates the ways in which African Muslims were brought to this country without nary a thought. SpearIt also highlights the importance of hip-hop not simply in religion understood broadly but also in religion according to the minister Louis Farrakhan. In his 2007 Saviours' Day speech Farrakhan argued this about hip-hop:

> Hip-hop is an art, and don't you talk down on it just because it has something in it that may not be to our liking. Talk up to it, because the hip-hop artist is the new leader. He leads the people wrong, but the same leader that leads them wrong can lead them right if you put the right message in their heads and in their hearts. Let's go get our hip-hop artists! Let's break the bond between these destructive CEO's and producers that tell conscious lyricists that that's not going to sell and force them to do filthy lyrics in the name of selling filth to our people. (Farrakhan 2007)

While some will readily dismiss Farrakhan because of some of his previous actions or statements as well as an abiding belief that he can do no good, he offers a compelling way to get out of the "hip-hop cannot be religious because of its unsavory elements" argument. He argues that hip-hop is an uplifting art and that it is often the capitalistic record companies that are pushing artists to produce unsavory music. The argument makes sense on its face. What possible incentive could there be to write a song about dancing in the club other than the $1 million a white music executive dangles in front of one's face. Hip-hop is a platform, and it allows people the opportunity to be heard who may have gone their whole lives not being acknowledged or listened to. Farrakhan argues that rather than reject hip-hop, we should recognize hip-hop artists as new leaders; even though artists are forced to make songs that are not in their or their community's interests, this does not mean that they aren't trying to help and uplift communities. He also urges a break from capitalistic practices, encouraging listeners to challenge who controls music production. This message resonated with people of many religious orientations who are often encouraged to reject the materialistic and antireligious positions of the status quo and invest in the religious values that one does hold dear. But as many Nation of Islam adherents will attest, when Farrakhan says it, it is somehow more dangerous or more offensive than if a similarly positioned white Christian leader were to say the same thing.

It is difficult to think about a hip-hop theology because of the diversity of religious beliefs in hip-hop. While eschatology and a desire to live a righteous life are popular themes, what constitutes that righteous life and how one should prepare for the end are debatable. There often seems to be a reverence for Jesus and God as well as the Islamic prophet Muhammad, but what that reverence entails and how it shapes hip-hop beyond the lyrics is not easy to discern. It could be that the music is just music; even though it takes up important religious ideas, it has little bearing on what an artist actually thinks or believes. In the same ways that rappers who have never robbed someone or who discuss poverty yet live in gated communities might rap about ideas that are quite different from their circumstances, so too might this happen with respect to religion.

Hip-hop's lasting influence will most likely be in the shaping of religious services. While Christian rap and religious-themed rap songs will no doubt remain popular, it will be the changing of traditional religious services that leaves a lasting mark. Perhaps it is too much to think about hip-hop as being equivalent to the translation of the Bible into the vernacular; it is a comparison worth making nonetheless. Churches became a lot easier to attend and were able to attract and maintain memberships when people could read the Bible and understand the preacher. Hip-hop may produce similar effects. We know that people have shorter attention spans and need chunking to better understand written materials. Church leaders could bemoan this and lament the decline of the written and spoken word, or they could accept it and think about hip-hop as a new way to make the religious message accessible. Accessibility should be an aspiration for the religious-minded, not something to trouble over.

Hip-hop and religion, like many other aspects of culture, are in a give-and-take. Hip-hop often contains religious themes even though the music might be nonreligious. It might take some time to find those songs, but religious scholars and people interested in hip-hop artists' religious ideas will be rewarded if they do. Christian hip-hop often gets derided by much of the hip-hop community, but although some may not find the content particularly interesting, the lyricism is definitely noteworthy. For all those people who dislike Christian hip-hop, I wonder whether they would hold the same opinion if they ignored the lyrics or tried to think beyond the God references.

Religion will remain a lasting influence on hip-hop because of religion's historical significance in the black community. Hip-hop will have a lasting impact on religion because it will continue to appeal to younger audiences and represent a new way to present religious messages to audiences unfamiliar with or uninterested in understanding traditional Bible verses.

Further Reading

Farrakhan, Louis. "Saviours' Day Speech." C-SPAN, February 25, 2007, www.c-span.org/video/?196795-1/savioursday-speech.
"Kurtis Blow, Worshipping through Hip-Hop." National Public Radio, December 19, 2006, https://www.npr.org/templates/story/story.php?storyId=6646367.
Lecrae. *Unashamed*. Nashville, TN: B&H Books, 2016.
Smith, Efrem, and Phil Jackson. *The Hip-Hop Church: Connecting with the Movement Shaping Our Culture*. Westmont, IL: InterVarsity, 2012.
SpearIt. "Sonic Jihad—Muslim Hip Hop in the Age of Mass Incarceration." *Florida International University Law Review* 11 (2015): 201–219.

Further Listening

Common. "Faithful," on *Be*. GOOD Music, 2005.
DMX. "Lord Give Me a Sign," on *Year of the Dog . . . Again*. Ruff Ryders, 2006.
Kanye West. "Jesus Walks," on *The College Dropout*. Roc-A-Fella Records, 2004.
Rakim. "Holy Are You," on *The Seventh Seal*. Ra Records, 2009.

CHAPTER EIGHT

The Arts and Hip-Hop

Hip-hop has also broadly affected the arts, including dance, painting, cinema, drama, and more. In part this should not be surprising. Music has often had a close relationship with other arts. Music has inspired painting, sculpture has inspired fashion, and dance has inspired cinema. The arts are generative. It is not simply that hip-hop creates art but that art also creates hip-hop. That is, influence is not a one-way street. Hip-hop has been instrumental in creating new styles of dance and encouraging branding that resembles graffiti work (e.g., car customizer West Coast Customs and Orlando restaurant Graffiti Junktion) as well as inspiring clothing styles from the likes of Burberry to True Religion. These are not important just for the black arts, although they certainly represent a valuable continuation of black artistic excellence. Rather, they have contributed broadly to art across racial lines. Graffiti appears in Barcelona and on t-shirts in Cape Town. Hip-hop dance happens in clubs in Osnabrück, Germany, and in Korean pop music. The flow of these artistic forms is thus a testament to hip-hop's influence.

One of the most interesting ways hip-hop has shaped the arts is its influence on painting. Obviously, graffiti has a broad impact. Graffiti is not just what appears on abandoned buildings and freight train cars, although it is certainly this too. Graffiti artists have been commissioned by cities and other organizations to create work. Sometimes graffiti is a way to bring the community together; graffiti has appeared behind (on the side opposite the Jade Museum) the Costa Rican National Museum in San Jose, Costa Rica, and on Atlanta's Greenbelt. One way that graffiti has helped public art is that it has drawn people's attention to public art creation. To be sure, some graffiti promotes gang activity, and people might reasonably debate the value of that art in a specific place, but graffiti has also helped people think about what space is and how we use it. Beyond graffiti, however, hip-hop has shaped the broad array of painting arts.

It is difficult to identify the beginning of hip-hop art. That term means many things and might include or exclude different types of visual arts. One person typically identified as a founder of hip-hop art is Jean-Michel Basquiat, the tragic figure of New York's urban art scene of the 1980s. Another origin story is that hip-hop art began with Lydia Yee and Franklin Sirmans's 2001 exhibition *One Planet under a Groove: Hip Hop and Contemporary Art* at the Bronx Museum of the Arts. The work brought together a multiracial cast of artists in a multiracial area to address the ascendant hip-hop's form. The show spanned works from Keith Haring to Sanford Biggers. This was less than 20 years ago, a very recent time in the history of art. But if asked whether black artists or hip-hop artists are important to art, many people might nod or make affirming noises as if of course these people were given their space in galleries or their pages in art history textbooks, yet those reactions probably are more defensive than reasonable analyses of the art scene.

One of hip-hop's pioneers, Fab 5 Freddy, was a noteworthy visual artist before he was one of the founding artists of hip-hip. Fab 5 Freddy connected the worlds of music and art in ways that would foreshadow later collaborations between rappers and visual artists, calling for the necessity of hip-hop as a holistic art form that could not be confined to one medium. He also laid the groundwork for hip-hop art that was not graffiti on train cars through his collaboration with Lee Quiñones. The exhibit of their work took place in 1979 in Galleria La Medusa in Rome and featured works on canvas. The move from train to canvas showed how hip-hop art was not confined to a certain medium, location, or even city.

Fab 5 Freddy's art was ensconced in the aesthetic of other artists whereby although he was a member of the Fabulous 5 graffiti crew he was also connected with other pop art movements, as evidenced by a 1980 project where he painted a subway train with Campbell's soup cans in homage to Andy Warhol. This seems almost kitschy now, but in 1980 it would have been shocking to evoke Warhol among graffiti artist–tagged train cars in New York City. Warhol was an artist of the Metropolitan Museum of Art, not the subway. His *Campbell's Soup Cans* had been made some 18 years before in 1962. The reference to Warhol was a sign that hip-hop artists were interested in the patterns of accepted art, and while their styles were divergent and original, they respected and drew from European and American art trends in a constant process of borrowing and remixing.

Jean-Michel Basquiat changed popular art such that it was increasingly acceptable for black artists to be adored if not respected by white audience. He was born in Brooklyn to a Haitian father and a Puerto Rican mother from Brooklyn. Basquiat's life was one of constant struggle. He eventually ran away from home and was homeless, yet after being homeless for only a short time he was soon selling paintings for $25,000, not an inconsequential sum now and certainly not in the late 1970s and early 1980s. Basquiat began working as a graffiti artist and was soon discovered while working under the pseudonym SAMO. Officially discovered in a group show, *The Times Square Show,* in July 1980, he soon had his first solo show in Modena, Italy, which opened on May 23, 1981. This soon led to shows in New York, southern California, and Italy. The cover of the rap single produced by Rammellzee, K-Rob, and Basquiat in 1983 featured his artwork. Basquiat was in many ways the darling of the contemporary art world, adored by white elites but never completely removed from the SAMO persona that began his career.

Basquiat struggled with sobriety much of his life, ultimately dying of a heroin overdose at age 27 in 1988. His death of course is a macabre moment of inclusion in the "famously dead at 27" group that includes Jimi Hendrix, Janis Joplin, Jim Morrison, Kurt Cobain, and Amy Winehouse. While not wanting to draw an unnecessary comparison, even Basquiat's death seems a connection to broader popular culture interest in the death of celebrities. Sometimes the connections are not intended but are nonetheless relevant.

For hip-hop personalities, art is political. That is not to indicate that art is not also for aural or visual pleasure but rather that art has a purpose beyond its uncritical consumption. The same interest that rappers had in challenging police misconduct, the drug war, and a lack of economic opportunity resonated with visual artists who took up the same ideas. Like their rapping counterparts, they also sought to challenge the sterilized, Eurocentric understanding of history. This is why many hip-hop artists draw on the history of slavery, the failures and opportunities of the civil rights movement, and the centrality of black empowerment in black progress.

Of course, Sanford Biggers would create much politically challenging art, including an untitled portrait in 2014 of a blond women wearing a Morehouse College T-shirt that challenged the ways we thought about historically black colleges and universities (HBCUs) and their relationship to white people including faculty, donors, and the community. At the time, as they are today, HBCUs are at the center of debates about black culture and education as well as the financial viability of HBCUs, given that many are experiencing decreased enrollment and the tightening of endowments. Biggers called for a direct confrontation with these ideas. His 2007 etched glass piece *Lotus* calls to mind the 1789 image of the *Brookes,* perhaps the most famous illustration of a slave ship. This image has of course also figured prominently in Hank Willis Thomas's *Absolut Power* (2003). By bringing the slave ship back to contemporary art (as if it ever left), artists demand that their audiences think through the troubling history of slavery that devalued black lives in the service of financial capital. Artists make history present visually, giving a visage of slavery's ever-present haunting. It is not that slavery isn't present but rather that artists such as Biggers and Thomas visually signify just how important slavery is to the present. This not only calls on black people to resist the degradations of slavery and its legacy but also asks white consumers to think about what they are viewing in art galleries and how their relationship to art is configured by slavery's legacy.

Hip-hop art's origin story matters less than developing an appreciation for the connection between hip-hop and art. Hip-hop music is of course art, but rather than focus on a specific date in the late 1970s or the creation of a specific painting at a specific time, it is important to understand that hip-hop music and hip-hop personalities do not exist in separate spaces from the rest of art. There is an open exchange. It is easy to trace the exchange from sampled sitar sounds or the opening rhythm from Egyptian pop star Sherine's (Shereen) "Al Sa'ban Aleh" (1980) in Fabolous and Ne-Yo's "Make Me Better" (2007), but it is much more difficult to isolate interactions between painting or sculpture and hip-hop music or break dancing. But it is also the case that international artists rely on hip-hop for music cues and dancing styles. The point, rather, is that hip-hop's influence is here regardless of where we place the origin.

Take for example Kehinde Wiley, the portraitist of President Barack Obama for the Smithsonian National Portrait Gallery. Wiley was born in Los Angeles and now spends much of his time in New York. On the surface, of course, this connection to the two biggest hip-hop centers of the United States provides an inevitable connection to hip-hop. Wiley is often grouped into the category of "hip-hop artists" because his art centers on black people and their relationship to the natural world. The portrait of Obama drew criticism for a number of reasons, including its use of vibrant colors. Color has been important to hip-hop since its beginning, from hip-hop fashion contesting the drab colors of white professional life to the association of colors with gangs and national origin. Wiley's painting *Judith and Holofernes* was the subject of much criticism because it showed a black woman holding the severed head of a white woman. The original painting *Judith Slaying Holofernes* was painted around 1614–1620 by Artemisia Gentileschi and has been painted by many other artists in various forms from Michelangelo and Caravaggio to Gustav Klimt. The paintings represent a story from the book of Judith. The opposition to Wiley's painting did not seem to be the violence or even the specific violence of a woman (Judith) toward a man (Holofernes). Rather, the opposition seemed to be that Wiley had depicted Judith as black, implicitly having committed violence against a white person. This centering of the black experience as powerful challenged the tired tropes of black subservience, shocking white audiences. That Holofernes had been sent to address the nations of the West refusing to support Nebuchadnezzar's reign makes the painting more disturbing to white sensibilities, as it positions a black women as metaphorically superior to the West. The audacity!

Recently, Art Basel's premier series of art shows in Basel, Miami, and Hong Kong featured a powerful sculpture by Hank Willis Thomas, *Raise Up,* featuring the raised arms of 10 black men invoking both the "hands up, don't shoot" message responding to the Michael Brown shooting in Ferguson, Missouri, and raising one's hands to the heavens to exalt a god. This work asked people to focus on the hands being raised, as the sculpture featured only the black people's arms and heads. Thomas has often critiqued capitalism, antiblackness, and other troubling social conditions. His work has spanned slavery, the civil rights movement, and the Black Power movement. The idea that Art Basel could feature prominent black artists seems hardly worth mentioning now, but 30 years ago major art shows in major world cities that featured black artists would have seemed preposterous. Thomas remarked in *The Guardian* that "Thirty years ago those would have been the signifiers that maybe you shouldn't be there" (Chang 2015), referencing the graffiti and black-centric art of Art Basel's 2015 Miami show. The event really was something radically different from what the art world had experienced and recast not only art but also what it meant to be a person in place.

Swizz Beatz, a hip-hop megaproducer, has openly embraced Art Basel, putting on a show with Bacardi titled *No Commissions*. The show toured in London, Shanghai, and New York. Swizz Beatz went from producing music for Jay-Z and DMX to putting on shows in the world's premier art cities. Swizz Beatz started the show as a way to give artists the ability to profit from their art without galleries taking substantial commissions on their work. In some ways this was a revolutionary idea, because it empowered artists and challenged the romantic notion of the starving artist. Indeed, one did not have to starve to make a living at art with Swizz Beatz's help. He also challenged the idea that there was something about art that wasn't hip-hop enough. While hip-hop culture had seemed to accept buying expensive homes, cars, and watches, buying art did not necessarily fit in. In this way, then, hip-hop has moved toward centering the artist, a problem in hip-hop's long history of artists versus record labels. It ought not be surprising, then, that there is a move to center and empower the artist.

Interestingly, it is not just hip-hop artists (rappers, producers, graffiti artists, etc.) buying hip-hop artists' work (painters, sculptures, etc.). Swizz Beatz recounts that the first expensive art he purchased was an Ansel Adams black-and-white photograph of the Alps. It would be difficult to conceive of a more mainstream and less exciting or shocking purchase. Adams, one of the best-know photographers in the world, is featured in galleries worldwide. His work is excellent but not seemingly hip-hop. This purchase indicates that hip-hop's impact on art is much more than about the production of various forms of art and is also about who consumes art. In many ways, most art collectors probably do not imagine Swizz Beatz as an equal or as a serious collector, yet this is exactly where we are in the contemporary art world. It seems that the way James Baldwin and Ralph Ellison challenged what good writing was (was it only the domain of white people?), so too are hip-hop artists challenging what the domain of art is.

Justin Bua is one artist whose prints have made waves across the world. *The DJ* is perhaps his most well-known work, a work that positions the DJ scratching on turntables, head bent to listen to a half-worn set of headphones, with the characteristic marks on the record to denote places for the DJ to start certain vocal or rhythm patterns and with a wall of records in the background. The DJ is adorned not with the flash of the rapper but instead with the workaday shabby chic of the DJ. The print best exemplifies what it is to be a DJ, to refine one's craft, and to lock out the rest of the world in pursuit of the right sound. Bua's work has appeared in the Los Angeles County Museum of Art and the Pop International Gallery in New York. What he has done for hip-hop art is make it accessible to the masses by pricing prints affordably and dealing exclusively in easily interpreted cityscapes and hip-hop life.

Hip-hop has blurred the line between high art/culture and low art/culture. As those familiar with debates in the arts before hip-hop will know, many have eagerly awaited this line blurring, while others have opposed it. Broadening the canon has allowed more students to experience more significant works and has also reduced the amount of time available for William Shakespeare or World War II. While some abhor these changes, if we can assume that expanding the field or discipline is a positive thing, then events such as the Art Basel shows have helped us better understand art as well as people who consume it and produce it.

Hip-hop has not erased the distinction between high and low culture, though. Even hip-hop fans will draw rigid lines between socially conscious or high hip-hop and party or low hip-hop. These divides mark Common as a different artist than 2 Chainz, and some fans will go so far as to argue that one cannot like one type of artist as well as another artist from a different type of hip-hop. This situation is analogous to debates in English literature about what constitutes literature. Can one read and enjoy Shakespeare and John Grisham or Chester Himes and Robin Cook? Anyone not heavily invested in these debates would obviously answer "of course." One can enjoy a filet mignon and also enjoy a backyard hamburger. One need not reject certain types of music, literature, or food to prove that one likes others.

As hip-hop continues its relationship with art, it will be interesting to observe what buying patterns are and if more rappers produce visual arts. Interesting studies of hip-hop art will focus on collecting as well as the relationship of artists to exhibits, galleries, and shows. This will change the way hip-hop art is understood as a version of pop art and will help foster an appreciation of hip-hop community members as being central to art's production, more so than the artists whose works white people purchase. The racial element, the association of hip-hop with blackness, is important and will continue to be important even as hip-hop diversifies and the community changes.

Jay-Z reminded everyone on 2017's "The Story of O.J." that "I bought some artwork for one million. . . . Few years later . . . worth eight million." Hip-hop arts were making serious investments in art because of a keen appreciation for art's value. Just like their white counterparts, art was not only something to value aesthetically but also something to value as an investment with an appreciable return.

Lest one think hip-hop has only influenced the visual arts, although this is certainly a place where hip-hops influence is strong, it has also influenced fashion in profound ways. The battle from the mid-1990s to the early 2000s involving Tommy Hilfiger, Ralph Lauren, and to a lesser extent Nautica was very much influenced by the clothing choices of hip-hop performers. One of the defining moments of the Tommy Hilfiger brand was when it openly embraced the hip-hop community, boosting Tommy Hilfiger to a a premier clothing line not simply for the upper middle class but also for the aspirant economically mobile hip-hop generation. Run-DMC's "My Adidas" made the shell-toe Adidas a mark of fashionability. Children and young adults by the thousands saved and stole to get those shoes in the 1980s, and now with the cyclical nature of fashion, hip-hop artists and shoe collectors, called "sneakerheads," still eagerly pursue original copies.

Run-DMC's legacy extends far beyond shoes. The group members regularly wore Kangol hats, wide shoelaces, and gold chains. The Kangol remained popular through the 2000s. Gold chains are still popular, although now they are often replaced with platinum chains. Wide shoelaces are still readily worn in hip-hop circles and also in the skater and surfing cultures, a testament to Run-DMC's broad public appeal.

Tupac worked for free as a model for Karl Kani, a prominent black designer. Karl Kani blended chic fashion with the colorful history of hip-hop. His shirts and other clothing items were known for their loud colors and today still look much the same.

Designers such as Dapper Dan produced not knockoffs but rather what came to be called "knockups" of Louis Vuitton and Gucci, among other elite designers. Dapper Dan's knockups were so expensive that only drug dealers and rappers could afford them. His styles outfitted Salt-N-Pepa and the Fat Boys, to name just a few. Dapper Dan made knockoffs acceptable and, in the remixing culture of hip-hop, repurposed corporate logos for his own ends, ultimately resulting in a federal raid of his boutique and its closure in 1992. Dapper Dan has now, coincidentally, partnered with Gucci to produce clothes, legally, under the Gucci–Dapper Dan label. The world has come full circle. Reminiscing about his journey through fashion, Dapper Dan explains that part of what he was trying to do was produce a lot with a little, a common theme in hip-hop whether it was using samples from other songs to produce a beat or figuring out how two cans of spray paint might be used to add depth and nuance to the letters on the side of an abandoned building. It seems that Dapper Dan is now mainstream, appearing on TBS's *Conan* in 2017. Dapper Dan helped instill in the hip-hop community an interest in exclusivity and high fashion that was not simply gold chains or big watches but was also about finely crafted and often one-of-a-kind clothes. His legacy lives on in the haute couture excess of hip-hop clothing where names such as Armani, Gucci, and Louis Vuitton are as common as they are at the country's high-end country clubs and vacation homes on Martha's Vineyard.

FUBU ("For Us By Us") also made waves in the fashion industry. Set up by Daymond John (who appears in the TV series *Shark Tank*), FUBU was originally all about directly serving the lower-income black community in New York. The brand sold over $200 million in merchandise in 1999, seven years after its creation. FUBU centered black creativity in black fashion in ways more direct than Karl Kani. The name of the FUBU label said it all. This label eagerly attracted LL Cool J, a hip-hop pioneer, and was selling across the country. Soon everyone from Russell Simmons to Jay-Z to P. Diddy would be deep in the fashion game, but the dominance of brands such as Sean Jean and Phat Farm would not last.

Now wearing these fashions is considered uncool, a signal that people are perhaps not classy or stuck in a bygone era. Today's hip-hop artists wear Givenchy, Armani, and myriad other high-end European brands. This is both a reaction to having to wear black designers because one could not afford anything else and a desire to be understood as powerful, wealthy, and just as good as other celebrities wearing exclusive clothes. Unfortunately, this means that many of the labels that made hip-hop fashion relevant have fallen into disrepair, and many black fashion designers and creatives are losing business to the Italian fashion houses whose clothing they never could have afforded 30 years ago and that would never have allowed the black designers' clothing in their boutiques.

Also, Nelly and the St. Lunatics produced a catchy and still present-in-the-club song called "Air Force Ones," referencing the Nike shoe by the same name. So popular was this style that one of the most popular artists in the 2000s made a song about them. The song is about different color shoelace combinations for this Nike shoe. Not surprisingly, the shoe continued to be popular after the song's release.

Many fashion innovations have their origin in hip-hop fashion. Oversized shirts still popular today were a product of hip-hop. Why? Opinions vary. Oftentimes artists of a lower socioeconomic standing had to wear a larger relative's clothes. The visual relationship between size and power signified by a bigger shirt was somehow representative of more power. Large shirts covered contraband and weapons better than tighter clothes. Sagging pants come from the plight of incarcerated individuals. Their pants sag because they cannot wear a belt in a holding cell; other conditions of confinement as well as prison uniforms also prevent access to belts. In this way, sagging one's pants was a show of solidarity with those who were incarcerated. Now pants sag with an exquisitely crafted leather belt, indicating that the original solidarity of the clothing choice may have given way to consumerism. These are just some of the examples of the lasting legacy of hip-hop fashion.

When OutKast rapped about being "so fresh and so clean," they were referencing the importance of appearance in hip-hop culture. The resiliency of many of these trends is striking. Sagging pants, Adidas sneakers, Nike sneakers, baggy clothes, and various forms of bling are all still central to hip-hop fashion. While hip-hop has trended toward tighter-fitting shirts and pants, a large segment of the population wears versions of clothes popular in the 1980, 1990s, and 2000s.

Hip-hop has also shaped dancing in a number of contexts. Perhaps most recognizable to the non–hip-hop audience will be R Kelly's "Bump n' Grind," which defined a certain form of dancing whereby partners would maintain close proximity to each other, with hips and rear ends locked in rhythmic movements. The song came out in 1994 and is still a feature at high school dances and in clubs to the present day. Hip-hop often encouraged not simply rhythm but also a physicality to dancing that was not common in disco or other popular dancing in the 1970s and 1980s. Other dances, of course, also began in hip-hop.

Some of these popular hip-hop dances and dance moves include much more than the break dancing of hip-hop's youth. Popping, locking, and krumping are all original styles of hip-hop dance that still power dance crews across the world. These styles challenge the idea that hip-hop dancing is only grindin' and that there are no complex moves associated with this form of dance. One of the great things about hip-hop dance is that anyone who wants to learn does not have to go to a club to do so; one can go to YouTube or even the local gym, where hip-hop workout and dance classes are increasingly popular. And it isn't just young people who are viewing these videos or attending these classes. The hip-hop dance craze is motivated a general belief that a lot of hip-hop culture is cool and that hip-hop dance may be physically enriching.

The Wobble is now a regular at weddings and picnics in much of black America. It began with Atlanta-based rapper V.I.C.'s "Wobble Baby," released in 2008. The dance is increasingly done in a group, as with the Cha Cha Slide and the Electric Slide. Videos on YouTube have countless great and less-than-great performances featuring stars and one's neighbors attempting the dance.

The Nae Nae, a reference to the character Sheneneh Jenkins in the TV series *Martin,* involves bent knees with a hand up toward the air and the other hand forward with palm facing the ground. Silentó's "Watch Me (Whip/Nae Nae)" popularized the move created a few years before by Atlanta group We Are Toonz. Now the Nae Nae can be seen in clubs, at tailgate parties, and on college campuses across the United States.

Twerking has been the subject of recent discussions beyond the hip-hop community. Twerking involves the moving of one's hips to accentuate and shake one's rear end. The result is that one's butt bounces up and down, and the larger one's butt, often the more impressive the results. The dance is popular in clubs, and a quick search of the Internet will yield countless results of people attempting to twerk. The dance gained popularity when the Ying Yang Twins released "Whistle While You Twurk" and received a further boost and caused an uproarious debate when Miley Cyrus posted a video of her twerking. The debate centered around the idea that twerking might be something that was a uniquely black form of dance and that the white Cyrus, always seemingly on the fringes of cultural appropriation, should not be increasing her fame by using this black form of dance. Other criticisms latched on to the idea that she was simply bad at twerking. These debates are important, though, because they ask people to consider what black art is and also ask whether the embracing of black art forms by white artists is homage or cultural appropriation. Those debates will not be resolved here, but understanding the complexity of shared culture means doing more than rushing to one's favorite social media platform and posting oneself or someone else attempting the latest hip-hop dance craze.

Other dances such as the Stanky Legg (GS Boyz's "Stanky Legg"), the Dougie (Cali Swag District's "Teach Me How to Dougie"), and the Harlem Shake (Baauer's "Harlem Shake") have been incorporated into countless how-to videos, dance routines, and rap songs. For example, G Dep's music video for "Let's Get It," featuring Diddy and Black Rob, also features the Harlem Shake prominently. While some of these dances may seem obscure, and the argument certainly is not that they have made their way into the corporate boardrooms and country clubs of the Midwest, they are nevertheless common in clubs and bars and at school dances much more than one might think.

Most recently, at the time of this writing the Shoot has been a popular dance based on BlocBoy JB's "Shoot." The dance features a prominently back-kicked leg and a hop-step. Again, videos abound with superstars from diverse fields and others trying to perform the move. In fact, Drake even attempts it in the video for "Look Alive." The move is so popular that Fortnite, the popular online videogame, even features the move. The song made the rounds in 2017 and is already one of the most popular dance moves in 2018, a testament to the viral nature of hip-hop and its ability to influence popular culture quickly.

Dance moves do not define hip-hop, but they do underscore the importance of controlling one's body, an important cultural theme. Keep in mind that the history of the United States has been about controlling bodies of color. Slavery involved excessive control over black bodies and regulated sleeping, standing, and all movements. Slaves were castrated, branded, and scarred. Black people could not sit, stand, or sleep in many places based on laws covering everything from watching movies to attending beaches. Black people were expected to act in certain ways, ways dictated to them by white people. Now it seems that black people cannot wear hoodies, drive cars, or use cell phones in their backyards. Black movement has always been policed. That whites are now interested in hip-hop dance is in some ways a corrective to the deeply troubling legacy of control over black bodies. It seems to be a corrective to the minstrel show, the popular shows where white people laughed at racist comedy that made fun of people of African descent. Those shows were designed to make fun of black people with racist generalizations. Now white people are actively trying to appropriate black culture, which while problematic seems to be motivated by a genuine appreciation for black culture. Although that motivation often produces racist results, the interest in hip-hop dance seems much more motivated by an appreciation for black artistic expression.

That hip-hop's influence extends far beyond music to encompass other arts is evidence that it is not only a musical form but is also a larger constellation of artistic expression. Hip-hop dance will continue to influence broader dance movements and be present at parties, dances, weddings, and in other venues where people get together to have a good time. Whether hip-hop dance will radically change how non–hip-hop community members dance remains to be seen. While there is some evidence to suggest influence, there is not the more sustained influence that is present in music. Likewise, hip-hop fashion will continue to influence fashion choices. Even as hip-hop artists embrace European fashion houses, it will still be these artists rather than Brad Pitt or George Clooney who help introduce Armani to the streets. The visual arts seem most clearly influenced by hip-hop, with graffiti and African tribal patterns well represented in traditionally white spaces and European tastemakers looking to black creativity for inspiration.

Further Reading

Chang, Jeff. "From Basquiat to Jay Z: How the Art World Came to Fully Embrace Hip-Hop." *The Guardian,* January 15, 2015, https://www.theguardian.com/culture/2015/jan/15/history-art-hip-hop-art-basel-miami-beach-kanye-jay-z-basquiat.

Lewis, Tasha, and Natalie Grey. "The Maturation of Hip-Hop's Menswear Brands: Outfitting the Urban Consumer." *Fashion Practice* 5 (2013): 229–243.

Murray, Derek Conrad. "Hip-Hop vs. High Art: Notes on Race as Spectacle." *Art Journal* 63 (2004): 4–19.

Further Viewing

Basquiat, Jean-Michel. *Irony of the Negro Policeman*. WikiArt, 1981. https://www
    .wikiart.org/en/jean-michel-basquiat/ironew-york-of-the-negro-policeman.
Basquiat, Jean-Michel. *Scull*. WikiArt, 1981, https://www.wikiart.org/en/jean
    -michel-basquiat/head.
Thomas, Hank Willis. *Absolute Power*. Artsy, 2003, https://www.artsy.net/art
    work/hank-willis-thomas-absolut-power.
Thomas, Hank Willis. *Raise Up*. Artadia, 2014, https://artadia.org/artist/hank
    -willis-thomas/hwt14-004_c-raise-up-hr/.
Wiley, Kehinde. *President Barack Obama*. Wikipedia, 2018, https://en.wikipedia
    .org/wiki/President_Barack_Obama_(painting)#/media/File:President
    _Barack_Obama_by_Kehinde_Wiley.jpg.

CHAPTER NINE

Politics and Hip-Hop

Politics has been a central concern for hip-hop since its inception. Hip-hop values black creativity and excellence and centers black people in politics, sociality, and expression. Black people have a long history of being political, of fighting for their equality against a political system that continued to degrade them and make them less than human. In the late 1970s and early 1980s there seemed to be relatively few political options for black people as well as other people of color in urban cities. There were not many people of color in national or state politics. Many old white power structures continued to govern cities. Barack Obama was an unknown. The legacy of the Black Power movement and the civil rights movement seemed uncertain given the war on drugs and the crack epidemic. Health inequalities and unfair policing were the norm. Campaigns to get out the vote were not robust.

Many of hip-hop's founders grew up while the civil rights and Black Power movements were happening or shortly after their end. Their parents, uncles, and aunts were often intimately familiar with these movements, having lived through them and experienced the depredations of the 1940s and 1950s. This time period both inspired hope and confronted people with a certain despair about the meaning of success. That is, even though various laws had been passed and advances seemed to have been made, many black people still suffered and lacked the fundamental necessities of life, including access to health care, a home, and a stable job. Oftentimes the civil rights movement is taught as a radical success story, one that enshrined a rights regime that universally empowered black people. Hip-hop community members knew that this was the whitewashed and white-empowering version of history, one that did not account for the complexities of civil rights and its unfinished legacy.

To fill in this gap between the radicalism of the Black Power movement and the dogged pursuit of electoral reform and the protection of voting rights by the civil rights movement, hip-hop advanced a radical black politics. This politics challenged the norms of civility and appropriateness, asked important questions about social and economic policy, and challenged white dominance in politics and corporations. Hip-hop's radical politics did all of these things at a time when it seemed as though black political participation and success might be rolling back to the years prior to the civil rights movement.

Much of hip-hop's early political importance stems from Public Enemy and N.W.A. Chuck D of Public Enemy famously proclaimed that "rap is black America's CNN." The message was simple: rap was informational and persuasive, and it filled a void that the current news landscape could not. Public Enemy's 11th album was titled *Most of My Heroes Still Don't Appear on No Stamps* (2012), a reference to "Fight the Power" that contained the line "most of my heroes don't appear on no stamps." The message was that postage stamps often contained pictures of slave owners and other people, often elected officials, who if not openly supportive of laws that disempowered black people were at least supportive of measures designed to curtail black freedom. These were not role models for black people, no matter how many teachers might try to convince students that George Washington and Woodrow Wilson should be idolized by black people. Chuck D and Public Enemy were challenging both who the government recognized on postage stamps as well as the way black children were being taught to value and idolize historic figures.

In the 1980s, hip-hop also turned international. Artists sharply critiqued apartheid in South Africa, and their involvement helped bring that racialized system of exclusion down. The 1985 release *Sun City* by Artists United Against Apartheid brought together rap, jazz, and rock heavyweights to critique Sun City, an exclusive resort that was used to lure artists to South Africa after the United Nations imposed a cultural boycott on the country for apartheid. The venue would host some of the recording industry's biggest names as the country's white elite forced the majority black population into increasing political irrelevance and subjected them to violent depredations. This is one example of the far-reaching political agenda.

Public Enemy took on debates surrounding Martin Luther King Jr. Day with "By the Time I Get to Arizona" (1991), which was a critique of Arizona's vote against establishing the federal holiday. Now the song seems to have foretold Arizona's harsh anti-immigration laws. In response to the statement of a signer of the petition against the holiday put forth by former Arizona governor Evan Mecham that "I guess King did a lot for the colored people, but I don't think he deserves a national holiday," which seemed to echo the opinion of many in Arizona. Chuck D called out both the racial politics of Mecham and the state's willingness to go along with politics as usual, as if Dr. King's work was no longer relevant in 1990. Now the song seems right on target, criticizing the devaluation of Mexican and Latinx persons who contribute financially, socially, and culturally to Arizona and states through-out the country. Politics as usual, though, counsels against recognizing the important diverse actors who have made the United States strong, and Arizona is leading the charge in seemingly criminalizing brownness. Other states have taken up similar anti-immigration laws, including Georgia, Indiana, and Alabama. Hip-hop seems to always be politically relevant no matter the time, region, people, or political controversy, as Public Enemy has for years proven.

Russell Simmons and Dr. Benjamin Chavis cofounded the Hip-Hop Summit Action Network in 2001 to politically engage hip-hop audiences in New York. The organization conducts meetings and symposia that bring hip-hop artists and their audiences together, encourages voting and other forms of political action, and promotes literacy, educational opportunities, and economic opportunity. In this way the organization channels much of the same ideas that animated the Black Power movement. This effort was mirrored in other locales with a focus on empowering young leaders. Hip-hop summits now occur regularly around the world, with artists' performance and political messaging affecting thousands of youths on nearly every continent. Efforts such as this help keep hip-hop listeners thinking about the political importance of hip-hop and their role in the political process.

Although resistance to police violence has readily been a theme for hip-hop artists, one of the best examples of this type of song is Wyclef Jean's "Diallo" (2000), which laments the 1999 New York Police Department's killing of unarmed Amadou Diallo, a young Guianese immigrant who was reaching for his wallet. Four plainclothes officers shot 41 times, claiming that Diallo had a gun. All officers were exonerated in the ensuing criminal trial. Wyclef sang "Who'll be the next to fire forty-one shots by Diallo's side?" His song went on to describe police officers as "vampires," depicting them as predators out for blood. So powerful was Wyclef's song that *New York Post* writer Dan Aquilante wrote that "there's no denying the ex-Fugee has created a protest song with the same backbone as anything Woody Guthrie, Pete Seeger, Bob Dylan, Bob Marley or Bruce Springsteen ever wrote to protest a perceived injustice" (Aquilante 2000). Obviously this is no small praise. Wyclef brought additional attention to one of the most heavily publicized police injustices of the era, a precursor to the protests against continued police misconduct that has killed Eric Garner, Tamir Rice, Walter Scott, and Freddie Gray, among countless others, encouraging many in the black community to argue for disbanding and disarming police departments because of seemingly weekly incidents of white police officers shooting black men.

Rapper Immortal Technique in a 2014 interview with VladTV argued that several reasons explain this behavior: police think they cannot be caught and believe that white life is worth more than black life and that rich life is better than poor life. Even if one is skeptical about these claims, one has to consider what they mean for folks who believe them. Hip-hop calls into question what it means to be black and what value this has relative to other races or peoples. If it is the case that white life is valued more—and there is evidence to support this claim coming from not simply the hip-hop world but also from sociology, economics, and other disciplines—then this also explains much of the hopelessness or fatalism in black culture. When those who are supposed to serve and protect do neither, the terms of existence are slanted away from black excellence. If it is also the case that rich lives matter more than poor lives, then many hip-hop artists who grew up black and poor are uniquely disadvantaged.

This is why hip-hop seems even more relevant now than it did in the early 2000s, when we knew that policing was discriminatory and that economic opportunities were unevenly distributed but did not have the visual confirmation that YouTube and other social media sites allowed. DJ Khaled's "Never Surrender" (2013) sounds a resilient theme that seems prevalent in modern hip-hop, bucking the more academic Afro-pessimism movements advanced by scholars such as Frank Wilderson and Jared Sexton. Indeed hip-hop, while not hopeful, seems to stress an ethic of perseverance. This is an important challenge to Afro-pessimism. The Afro-futurist perspective that envisions a world where black excellence and opportunity are possible is promoted by artists such as OutKast, Missy Elliott, and Afrika Bambaataa. The Afro-pessimist and Afro-futurist perspectives are prominent in black political thought and have been the focus of countless articles and books. Hip-hop artists are invested in both positions and a plethora of other positions that run the gamut of pessimist, hopeful, and optimistic political orientations.

Furthermore, Drake opposed offshore drilling with a performance in 2000 at the 9:30 Club in Washington, D.C., in many ways expanding hip-hop's political focus. While environmental protection and power production are clearly issues that affect all people, hip-hop had focused elsewhere. Yet Drake, a Canadian rapper who was world famous, lent his voice in support of this effort—no doubt a testament to hip-hop's far-reaching political program.

With the rising emphasis on border security and the exclusion of black and brown bodies from the United States, Talib Kweli released "Papers Please" to challenge Arizona's anti-immigration law. The law, in the vernacular, would allow law enforcement officials to ask for a person's papers (legal documents indicating their citizenship status), with little to no pretense. Obviously the law impacted Latinx populations in the United States, especially Mexicans in the Southwest. The law's impact on black persons would probably be lesser than the impact on brown persons, but of course black persons with accents were at risk of having their citizenship challenged.

Jadakiss has released two of the more politically powerful songs, "Why" and "Jason." "Why" challenged the presidency of George W. Bush, asking "Why did Bush knock down the towers?" The line clearly evokes blame for

Bush's and other Republicans' oppressive politics toward the Middle East. While the conspiracy theories about Bush's involvement in the terrorist attacks of September 11, 2001, are many, Jadakiss's point is that it is precisely the destructive politics of Republican leaders that have decimated the Middle East in a never-ending war of changing allegiances as the U.S. government has ham-handedly tried to support whoever it thought would best benefit the United States. "Why" focused a critical eye on media and presidential politics. The music video showcased war scenes and "hanging chads."

Jadakiss also critiques the criminal justice system with biting lines such as "why they gotta open your package and read your mail" and "why they stop letting brothers get degrees in jail," a critique of the decrease in funding for GED and other educational programs at the nation's prisons as well as the loss or privacy for inmates. Both are substantial curtailments of prisons' ability to rehabilitate inmates, as prisoners are neither treated like humans nor provided opportunities to better themselves. The problem, in short, isn't just discriminatory policing practices but also the lack of opportunity once policing occurs. We have given up on rehabilitation as a goal of punishment such that punishment seems only to be retributive, at least according to much of the hip-hop community. Understood this way, Jadakiss's criticisms seem well placed. If overpolicing cannot be solved, then at least the hip-hop community can ask for opportunities in jail so that they might fight not to return.

Likewise "Jason," released prior to Halloween in 2015, drew on both Halloween themes and the danger that police pose to black people. The song evoked the idea of masked violence and fear and, in its black-and-white display, suggested the complex relationship and stark opposition between white and black people. The repeating of "Don't shoot, can't breathe" was an allusion to Eric Garner, who was killed by a police choke hold. Jadakiss also connects this criticism to criticism of the Central Park Five, a group of black and Latino youths falsely accused of a brutal attack of a white woman and others in Central Park in 1989. Jadakiss raps "I'm just one of the five," connecting the precariousness of his position as a black man to the constant threat of systematic racism and discriminatory policing. Jadakiss's white hoodie contains the all-caps phrase "DO SOMETHING," urging the audience to not simply tweet or blog about injustice and instead leave the comfort of their homes and cell phones, go out into the world, and attempt to change it.

The Jadakiss example might seem inconsequential, but it is this micropolitics of resistance that makes hip-hop so important. Not every lyric or every song or every album needs to change the world for hip-hop to be an engaging cultural act. Hip-hop artists, like authors and painters, do not produce great work every time, and this should be acceptable in a critical thinking public. However, oftentimes fickle observers and a vitriolic social media atmosphere have difficulty seriously engaging hip-hop's many artists. Hip-hop is hard work.

Hip-hop artists are using their platform to critique police violence. The effect of this will be difficult to determine. Surely hip-hop will expose more people to critiques of police violence, but it is unclear what impact this will have beyond the already widespread coverage of police violence across social media as well as traditional news outlets. Hip-hop's interest in issues that affect its communities is admirable and certainly moderately consciousness-raising, but it seems unlikely that hip-hop will radically alter the way communities of color regard police.

It is not just black artists calling out white power structures. Eminem, considered by many to be one of the greatest (white) rappers in history, argued in a 2017 cipher that Donald Trump's racism and threat to the United States was so great that he felt obligated to call out the injustices he saw: "And any fan of mine who's a supporter of his, I'm drawing in the sand a line, you're either for or against." Eminem's message is clear.

President Trump and other politicians have engendered much criticism from the hip-hop community. Joey BadA$$'s "Land of The Free" (2017) is a succinct historicization of the present political program, commenting that "Obama just wasn't enough. . . . And Donald Trump is not equipped to take this country over." BadA$$'s argument evokes both the need to wake up to the injustices of the present, a problem not only for white Americans who supported Trump but also for people of color still living in the afterglow of the Obama presidency. BadA$$'s reference to 300 years of cold shoulders evokes slavery, Jim Crow, and the legacy of racism. He also argues that Obama indeed did not solve racial inequality. Many hip-hop artists have argued that assuming that Obama would solve racial inequality was a farce to begin with. BadA$$'s cliffhanger is the unstated motive for Trump's presidency, which he evokes in other lines of the song and to which the music video testifies, namely racism. Rap such as this aggressively challenges those in power, thus shaping, by giving a new vocabulary, the political consciousness of many of today's youths and of those who grew up with much older hip-hop and maintain an interest in the culture.

If one were to conceptualize a hip-hop political platform, the platform would certainly be left of center. The majority of hip-hop artists, assuming their voting rights haven't been taken away through systematic felon disenfranchisement, vote Democratic. Hip-hop artists support broader and better health care, checks on policing, vaguely socialist economic positions, prison reform or abolition, legalization of some drugs, harsher penalties for snitching, and reinstating the voting rights of felons. These positions are often in keeping with traditional Democratic politics, although they are often framed as issues important to people of color specifically. Many hip-hop artists advocate for increased educational opportunities in inner cities and prisons as well as reforms to curricula that offer Afro-centric education and emphasize black accomplishment.

Hip-hop's enduring influence will be that it critiques policies detrimental to people of color. Hip-hop will also increase education about social ills and provide valuable political commentary that many people of color miss in nightly news coverage and in public school. These messages will not be earth-shattering to many communities of color but will lend support to many of their ideas about politics. Hip-hop artists will continue to advance messages of equality and critiques of capitalism, white supremacy, and the uneven distribution of social services. These messages will resonate with hip-hop's core audience of youths of color in urban areas. Hip-hop will also expose people to issues that they do not deal with or might not think about regularly. Many hip-hop artists will encourage social activism, protest, and voting. These agenda items will advance the cause of many and continue to push hip-hop's political agenda.

Further Reading

Aquilante, Dan. "Wyclef Jean Takes a Shot at Diallo Tale." *New York Post,* August 22, 2000. https://nypost.com/2000/08/22/wyclef-jean-takes-a-shot-at -diallo-tale/.

Ogbar, Jeffrey O. G. *Hip-Hop Revolution: The Culture and Politics of Rap.* Lawrence: University Press of Kansas, 2007.

Stapleton, Katrina R. "From the Margins to the Mainstream: The Political Power of Hip-Hop." *Media, Culture & Society* 20 (1998): 219–234.

Vito, Christopher. "Who Said Hip-Hop Was Dead? The Politics of Hip Hop Culture in Immortal Technique's Lyrics." *International Journal of Cultural Studies* 18 (2015): 395–411.

Further Listening

Artists United Against Apartheid. "Sun City," on *Sun City.* EMI, 1985.

Immortal Technique. "The Poverty of Philosophy," on *Revolutionary Vol. 1.* Viper Records, 2001.

Jadakiss. "Jason," on *Top 5 Dead or Alive.* D Block, 2015.

Jadakiss. "Why," on *Kiss of Death.* Ruff Ryders, 2004.

Public Enemy. "Fight the Power," on *Fear of a Black Planet.* Def Jam, 1990.

Epilogue

There are new avenues of hip-hop study and also ways in which, and areas where, hip-hop will remain a vital part of popular culture. No matter what one's education or employment status, family structure, or musical preferences, hip-hop is out there. It is going to be difficult to avoid. Rather than complain about the offensive lyrics, which has proven to be an ineffective strategy for combating the ills of hip-hop since C. Delores Tucker's public battle against Tupac Shakur, it pays to understand the influence that hip-hop has. The best critics and the best criticism are grounded in understanding influence rather than fear and hate. In part, then, this book is geared toward generating not an uncritical appreciation for hip-hop but rather a critical and nuanced engagement with hip-hop.

There is a strong case for hip-hop's influence on popular culture, its importance to different ways of thinking and different life experiences, and its role in academic discussions and the way we teach and learn. The business of hip-hop means that advertising, trends, and business ventures will increasingly take into account what hip-hop artists and community members want and do. It means that people in many different types of jobs will need to become increasingly aware of issues ranging from public use to freedom of expression to social media. One's accountant may need to learn about royalties, and one's lawyer may need to brush up on what constitutes a threat. If one is an accountant, one may need to revisit revenue streams and what constitutes business expenses. One's children may seek to model hip-hop styles of dress and may desire to experience a hip-hop concert as a birthday gift. One's thesis supervisor may play Public Enemy in their office more than Bob Dylan. As trite as the notion of times changing is, hip-hop has had a lasting influence and is as popular as ever.

Of course, one can try to hide from hip-hop or lessen its influence. Monitoring what one's children listen to or what websites they access would be one such strategy. While hip-hop is a global phenomenon, one could try to move away from urban areas to less diverse and less dense cities, towns, and counties to lessen the likelihood of experiencing hip-hop. People do these sorts of things regularly, from only consuming news with a certain political angle to only shopping at certain stores. Perhaps we will witness population moves to resist hip-hop in the same ways that people turn off jazz radio stations or fast-forward through objectionable movie scenes, but there is little indication that this is likely or that it is happening in any real sense. For better or worse, hip-hop artists have even taken up the messages of some of its critics, as evidenced by Baked Alaska's "MAGA Anthem" (2016) as well as Christian hip-hop. While these types of hip-hop are often derided as cultural appropriation or just plain bad music or not hip-hop, they demonstrate the appeal to groups and people who often malign hip-hop. If one embraces a cultural form to serve one's ends, then one has implicitly argued that this cultural form is relevant and is likely effective in some sense.

Kanye West's recent Twitter promotion of Donald Trump has raised serious questions about what political commitments hip-hop artists should have. Some have argued that Kanye's tweets should be understood in light of his addiction to opiates as well as his depression and bipolar disorder and the stress of being a star. Others have argued that there simply is no good reason for Kanye, a black man who many people of color look up to, to demonstrate support for a president who seems determined to actively destroy people and communities of color. John Legend has been a harsh critic of Kanye. Despite this, Kanye has consistently argued that people are allowed to have different opinions, and Chance The Rapper has emphasized that all black people do not have to be Democrats. These points are reasonable enough, but they miss the importance of what one's opinions and political orientations mean for people and how they affect one's followers and the millions of people of color who take very seriously what hip-hop artists say. As hip-hop artists increasingly voice political opinions in public forums such as Twitter, Instagram, and other social media platforms, we are likely to be exposed to a wide array of political ideologies. We know that many artists supported George W. Bush, and although many later regretted it, their support is certainly noteworthy. The question about party alignment is in some ways a red herring. It does not much matter if hip-hop artists are part of any specific political group, but it does matter what political positions they advance given their large followings. What matters is not just the millions of albums, downloads, and streams for which they are responsible but also their followers on social media. Because hip-hop artists are often role models for community members and people the world over, they have a duty to the people who look up to and follow them. A well-articulated, thoughtful political position is always defendable, but sometimes even a defendable position is not the best position for oneself or the people one helps and influences. Time will tell what we do with Kanye's seeming support of Trump, but it is unlikely that

Kanye will become less relevant and likely that he will become more disliked.

Compounding this confusion, Kanye recently stated in an interview that slavery seemed like a choice. It is difficult to unpack what this means in a world where we know people do not chose to be slaves and where numerous slave rebellions, revolts, and protests occurred in seemingly every state where there were slaves in the United States. For every time that hip-hop might be applauded for challenging whitewashed history present in many United States textbooks, there are times when hip-hop artists are simply wrong. Rapper B.o.B. recently got into a feud of sorts with Neil deGrasse Tyson over B.o.B.'s insistence that the Earth is flat or at least could be. There seems to be some debate over the strength of his claim. Quite obviously, because of science we know that the Earth is round. We know that the Earth is round because of countless data points and well over 1,000 satellites in space. We have also known that the Earth is round for approximately 2,000 years. So convinced is B.o.B. that he started a GoFundMe page to raise money to put a satellite in space to test whether or not the Earth is flat. What that satellite will do that others have not is confusing at best. Hip-hop artists make mistakes—some of them defy even the most basic understanding of the world—but there are actually quite a few flat-earthers in the world, so having one semiprominent hip-hop artist espousing this belief is not particularly noteworthy.

Likewise Killer Mike, who campaigned heavily for Bernie Sanders during the 2016 presidential campaign, caused a commotion when he was interviewed on NRA TV and seemed to advocate for gun rights. Killer Mike's comments were largely taken out of context, as his point was that black people need to arm themselves to protect themselves from white supremacy, which is a position consistent with many members of the Black Panther Party and others associated with the Black Power movement. Yet, the National Rifle Association (NRA) won the spin battle and made it seem like Killer Mike wanted everyone armed for fear of their guns being taken away by some unknown and unthinkable government agent. Killer Mike lost some fans for these comments and was widely condemned by public intellectuals. He later apologized particularly in light of the National School Walkout when students walked out of school in support of increased gun control. His statement, shot before the National School Walkout, urged his children to stay in school, which seemed to be a point about the importance of participating in school more than it was a rejection of the walkout. Here again, though, a hip-hop star who had made tremendous political strides in the last year or so put all of that in jeopardy by expressing a poorly constructed argument. Had Killer Mike better constructed his argument to indicate that education was important and that the protest was an opportunity cost (e.g., one can't learn in the classroom while out of it), then he likely would have faced less criticism. He didn't word that argument well, and it hurt him and cast doubt on his commitment to the protection of black lives in a country where structural racism makes it difficult to be black anytime and anywhere. The Killer Mike story is a story about the difficulty of expressing oneself, given that white people often seem obsessed with finding any evidence that a black person might not be perfect or might be capable of complex thought that is therefore manipulable. This is as much the NRA's fault as it was Killer Mike's fault, but Killer Mike did himself no favors.

There are repercussions to political expression, which may explain why many hip-hop artists have not used their stardom and followers to enter politics. Rather, hip-hop artists seem content to make music, much of which is not overtly political. This is a relatively safe position, as it promises to avoid political controversy and provide, at least theoretically, a path to financial freedom. Further study of hip-hop artist political participation should consider the number of political opinions expressed as well as the degree of political affiliation (very Democratic, reverently supportive of gun control, etc.). It would be interesting to follow those opinions as they change, strengthen, and weaken as hip-hop artists achieve stardom, age, and become more active on social media or sell more records.

For young people interested in hip-hop who think that the cars and watches provide some sort of greater life, weigh that $5,000 watch against a semester or year in college or several months' rent. Sometimes putting things in perspective can help students learn and embrace hip-hop in meaningful ways. Sure, buy the expensive watch, but when one cannot afford to go to college next year, remember the choice that was made. Students are usually quite able to comprehend life's trade-offs, and this can also be a way to expose where hip-hop might display a false image. If we know that an artist has not released an album, is not a household name, and does not have any other significant source of income, then we can reason that the expensive watch in the music video is borrowed, leased, or even a knockoff. Thinking through hip-hop in these ways can help young people understand their priorities. It is also a corrective to the promotion of hip-hop's automatic wealth and stardom, which still permeates many listeners and young artists.

There is much work to be completed on hip-hop. Artists and community members are increasingly the subject of biographies and documentaries. Yet, hip-hop community members still need more control over the means of production. Rather than beg banks for loans or depend on often rich white moguls, hip-hop community members must pursue community-based funding options so that they do not lose artistic control of their products. In order to better understand hip-hop, scholars, community members, and activists will need more explorations of specific hip-hop artists (biographies, autobiographies, and documentaries) as well as sustained study of particular events (artist feuds, community outreach, awards shows, etc.). Of course, there are many newer artists who deserve scholarly attention such as Chance The Rapper, Kendrick Lamar, and A$AP Rocky.

The next wave of hip-hop scholarship will likely consider these artists and others like them who are pushing the boundaries of hip-hop delivery and rhyme schemes while also producing extremely social justice-oriented lyrics. Hip-hop fans complaining about how hip-hop has lost its way with too much trap music are likely to find a lot to interest them in the work of rappers such as Chance and Kendrick. The social justice roots of hip-hop are also not going away. For every party track, there is someone rapping about police brutality. Systemic inequality exists, and absent a complete overhaul of the economy, people of color will continually be disadvantaged. This inequality will inspire creativity, and some of that creativity will create beautiful music and murals. Sometimes people forget how resourceful people can be, and oftentimes the resourcefulness of populations that are not valued by large segments of society are denigrated or ignored. Hip-hip is doing a lot of good now and will continue to do good to the extent that it addresses problems in the world and provides opportunities for people to share their views and take solace in their communities.

The greatest thing about hip-hop is that so many fantastic artists are making music now that it is easy to find their music. This is also hip-hop's worst curse—there are so many artists, many not very good, who are producing music. The field is crowded, and one can still walk through Hollywood and be accosted by artists selling CDs for $5 or $10. It would be impossible for any listener, scholar, or DJ to stay up-to-date on all the new artists, controversies, or gossip. This keeps hip-hop interesting. It is always fresh. No matter where one is in the world, there are new artists and new sounds. More so, one always risks being out of style, behind, or out of touch, which is a great motivator to investigate, buy music, and download new content. This is one reason why people stay interested in hip-hop—it is always changing, and there is always something to be discovered.

This also explains why hip-hop remains important in culture. There are always new products, clothing styles, and commentaries on public affairs. Hip-hop is polyvocal. This means that people will continue to come into contact in different ways and different places. They will hear hip-hop on Capitol Hill in Washington, D.C. (where many artists have testified before Congress on a number of issues), as well as in small towns in Africa. We are also experiencing a revitalization of what was once considered old. Rappers such as Chuck D, who led Public Enemy, are so active on Twitter that younger hip-hop heads who may have only vaguely known about Public Enemy are now investigating this groundbreaking group because of Chuck D's social media politics and not at all because of Flavor Flav's role on *The Surreal Life, Strange Love,* and *Flavor of Love,* all of which also increased interest in Public Enemy.

As hip-hop changes, expands, and contracts, scholars must address these flows, recognizing the larger changes in culture. What is popular or influential today may not be so tomorrow. Historical memories are often short. So, while it may be sacrilegious to suggest that Public Enemy or N.W.A. may become less important, 20 years from now those artists who thrust hip-hop into national recognition may no longer have the following or be understood as important. M. K. Asante Jr. makes such an argument when he describes the post–hip-hop generation of hip-hop community members who lack experience with the 1980s and 1990s as a reference point for their participation in hip-hop. Even today, first-year college students may have been born after September 11, 2001. This means that they will be much more familiar with Drake than with Common. They will only know the Roots as Jimmy Kimmel's live band and not for their socially conscious hip-hop. Those born after 9/11 will know how to use Photoshop and other graphic design programs to do graffiti but are unlikely to have ever held a can of spray paint. They will know about computer programs to mix music but may have never seen a dual-cassette boom box. Changes in technology and historical knowledge are not a death knell for hip-hop but instead point to the complexities of technology and popular taste.

Much like Annales school scholars sought to work on big history, so too will hip-hop scholars need to develop strategies to trace hip-hop over decades and continents given changing economic conditions, artistic norms, political strategies, and the like. It is common in scholarly discourse to talk and write of the *longue durée,* or the long era. This approach does not examine discrete time periods more so than it appreciates that the story of history is long and does not have definite starting and ending dates. It is easy to indicate that the American Civil War started when South Carolina seceded from the Union and ended at Appomattox Court House, but the Civil War was caused by slavery that had existed for many years before South Carolina seceded, and Reconstruction and Jim Crowism continued many of the debilitating effects of slavery. Some more radical scholars argue that the Civil War is still going on or that we are at least still experiencing its effects. Hip-hop scholars will need to work in this tradition, not confining themselves to the hip-hop generation or the post–hip-hop generation. Hip-hop has its roots in Africa and is clearly connected with the social politics of black radicalism in the 1950s and 1960s. Hip-hop did not discreetly begin at a house or block party and will not end with a certain act or certain hip-hop/pop crossover. Every time a hip-hop artist does a song with a pop star or a country star, as with the poorly received Nelly and Tim McGraw song "Over and Over" (2004), this sounds the bell for hip-hop being dead. But hip-hop's experimentation with other artists and types of music certainly does not mean that it is dying, no matter how harshly some fans may react to those collaborations.

Lest hip-hop studies be understood as applicable only to hip-hop, scholars will need to continue applying hip-hop beyond its musical form. Lawyers and legal scholars will become aware of hip-hop theories of justice, mass incarceration, and discrimination because law clerks and clients and increasingly judges and senior partners will become aware of the exchange between law and hip-hop. We will continue to revisit ideas of fair use and copyright in a sharing economy. As language patterns change, managers and English teachers will need to think through how they plan to deal with people who don't speak and write the King's English. Hip-hop's history will grow longer and more complex. Historians will have to consider not only the 1980s and 1990s but also the influence of regional hip-hop styles and the rise and fall of labels such as No Limit Records. Business leaders will need to consider how to appeal to the hip-hop community even if they do not sell clothing or lifestyle products. Real estate agents will need to connect with hip-hop community members looking for certain neighborhood attributes or architectural styles. There will be much more work to do.

There does not seem to be a point on the horizon where hip-hop is no longer a part of popular culture. Even with quickly changing musical and art preferences, hip-hop has demonstrated a salience that is unlikely to dissipate. If hip-hop is understood as only a music form, then people risk dismissing it as nothing more than a fad, in the way that jazz and other musical forms were often demeaned. Hip-hop is firmly entrenched in academia, business, and just about every aspect of culture. It is visual, aural, and oral. It stimulates the senses. It calls attention to social ills and issues that matter not just for hip-hop musicians or community members but all individuals. It is not going away.

It is easy to dismiss advances in the study of culture as just a fad or trend, and this is often a first response to a new cultural form. It is easy to dismiss hip-hop as low art, reinforcing the low art/high art divide that has plagued much of cultural studies. But rather than try to decide what kind of art hip-hop is, it is more worthy of our time to accept it as art and culture and think about what this means for how we live our lives. When J. Cole raps "You hate it before you played it. I already forgave ya," he's expressing a powerful idea about the dangers of a closed mind and the effect this can have on the ability to appreciate difference and newness. J. Cole has been one of the more popular recent artists in hip-hop, but he does have his fair share of haters. He argues that even though people are quick to make snap judgments, this is not a reason to hate someone. In fact, so natural are these judgments that forgiving someone is the only natural response. If human nature is such that we will always judge, oftentimes based on limited evidence, then the only ethical response is to be as charitable as possible with those who are ill-informed. This is one of hip-hop's virtues that often gets denied in the face of beefs, rivalries, and highly publicized conflicts. Many hip-hop artists understand that conflict is a necessary part of life and that conflict does not preclude meaningful thought, revaluation, or change. J. Cole's words underscore this.

Returning to Nas's idea that hip-hop is dead raises the question of what we want from hip-hop. Hip-hop cannot solely be the underground phenomenon it was in the late 1970s and early 1980s in Brooklyn and the Bronx. Hip-hop has grown and matured and spread across the world, and those artists who started hip-hop are in a different place lyrically, politically, and generationally than they once were. It is irresponsible to argue that hip-hop is dead, but it is not irresponsible to argue that hip-hop has changed. Hip-hop is big business, embraced not as a counterculture but rather as a significant part of culture. Forty years ago the idea of a white man in Iowa City listening to hip-hop would have been met with uproarious laughter, but today it happens in Iowa City and Mexico City, Senegal and South Africa, and China and Moscow. People are listening to and making hip-hop in new and exciting ways. While we can reminisce about the importance of DJs actually using turntables or worry about the authenticity of a graffiti-inspired T-shirt sold at Target, today's changes in hip-hop are a sign that the great work done in hip-hop for decades meant something and continues to mean something. Arguing that hip-hop changed is a much better way to think about hip-hop's evolution than to argue that hip-hop is dead. In fact, one might reasonably conclude that the emphasis on club music as opposed to the rich lyrical content of N.W.A. and Public Enemy actually takes us back to hip-hop's earliest days, when it was designed to get people dancing in the streets. The rhythms and beats may have changed even though artists continue to sample music from R&B artists and early hip-hop, but the goal of bringing people together to have fun has not changed.

President Barack Obama was hailed as the hip-hop president, although what that meant is not quite clear. He did admittedly like many hip-hop artists and often listened to them on his iPod; he also invited many to perform in official government functions. But President Obama did not radically change racial politics in the United States. Many people of color remain upset at how little he did for people of color as he moved to the center on many important issues, not unlike many presidents before him. At no other time has hip-hop been so prominently featured in a country's national politics. Obama drew much criticism from right-wing commentators for his hip-hop interests, but he also encouraged an ongoing dialogue about what hip-hop meant in the world. Even if he did not change racial politics in the ways that supporters hoped for, he did get more people thinking about hip-hop, even those predetermined to hate it and him for it.

Further Reading

Frere-Jones, Sasha. "Rapping It Up." *New Yorker,* March 8, 2004, https://www
.newyorker.com/magazine/2004/03/08/rapping-it-up.

Reynolds, Simon. "Hip-Hop: Notes on the Noughties." *The Guardian*, November 26, 2009, https://www.theguardian.com/music/musicblog/2009/nov/26/notes-noughties-hip-hop.

Further Listening

Damien Marley and Nas. *Distant Relatives*. Universal Republic, 2010.
Nas. "Hip Hop Is Dead," on *Hip Hop Is Dead*. Def Jam, 2006.

Index

About the Author

Dr. Nick J. Sciullo is an assistant professor of communications at Texas A&M University–Kingsville. In 2018, he was recognized as the Forensic Educator of the Year by the Argumentation and Forensics Division of the Southern States Communication Association. In 2016, he was awarded the Best Dissertation Award by the Critical & Cultural Studies Division of the National Communication Association. Sciullo has been published in dozens of peer-reviewed journals and law reviews on issues of rhetoric, race, class, and law. He has also spoken on hip-hop across the United States and Western Europe.